Strategic Weapons:

An Introduction

Norman Polmar

PUBLISHED BY

Crane, Russak & Company, Inc.

NEW YORK

National Strategy
Information Center, Inc.

Strategic Weapons:
An Introduction

Published in the United States by
Crane, Russak & Company, Inc.
347 Madison Avenue
New York, N.Y. 10017

Copyright © 1975 The Churchill Press, Inc.
5205 Leesburg Pike
Falls Church, Va. 22041

Library Edition: ISBN 0-8448-0822-9
Paperbound Edition: ISBN 0-8448-0823-7
LC 75-34511

Strategy Paper No. 27

Printed in the United States of America

Table of Contents

Preface

This monograph seeks to fill a longstanding need for an outline of the development of strategic weapons and a description of their basic characteristics. Such an effort must suffer the severe limitations of brevity required in a monograph. Still, it is hoped that the volume will serve the purpose intended.

The definition of a strategic weapon is not easily derived. The US Department of Defense *Dictionary of Military and Associated Terms* (JCS Publication 1) does not even list the term. A definition can, however, be extrapolated from the volume's definition of "strategic mission":

> A mission directed against one or more of a selected series of enemy targets with the purpose of progressive destruction and disintegration of the enemy's warmaking capacity and his will to make war. Targets include key manufacturing systems, sources of raw materials, critical materials, stockpiles, power systems, transportation systems, communication facilities, and other such target systems.

The concept of strategic warfare is not new. The Roman destruction of Carthage, and sowing salt on the ground where it stood to destroy its fertility, absolutely ended the capacity of an enemy to make war. In the era of sailing ships, the Royal Navy was a strategic weapon, employed to blockade an enemy nation and destroy its seagoing commerce, in addition to fighting its navy. Similarly, in World War II the US and German submarine fleets, and the US and British bomber forces, had primarily strategic rather than tactical missions. In the post-World War II period, however, the term "strategic" has become synonymous with weapons of mass destruction. And, in the context of modern long-range missiles and nuclear warheads, the definition of strategic missions and hence weapons must be expanded to include the destruction of an enemy's strategic weapons in certain scenarios. In addition, certain tactical weapons—those that can strike an enemy homeland—must be discussed in the context of strategic weapons.

If the definition of strategic weapons is inexact, so is the information traditionally available from open sources. During the past few years, however, the debate in the United States over defense policies has led to the release of an unprecedented amount of information. This information has appeared in publications that receive very limited distribution (such as hearings of Congressional subcommittees, which are not reprinted in the widely distributed *Congressional Record*), and in speeches before specialized groups.

Strategic Weapons: An Introduction provides an abbreviated discussion of US and Soviet strategic weapons development—both the rationale for their development and the weapons themselves. An effort has been made to keep the discussion nontechnical. Still, the "hardware" must be described. Their existence or nonexistence, and not necessarily the rationale for their development or nondevelopment, must be a primary consideration for those interested in national strategic policies.

The discussion is chronological to the extent possible, beginning with the detonation of the first nuclear weapons in 1945. Strategic weapons development is primarily the history of US and Soviet efforts. But because the impact of nuclear weapons development in other nations could be increasingly important in international affairs, a brief chapter on The Other Nuclear Powers is included.

Jargon has been kept to a minimum, and a Glossary of Terms is provided. The term "weapon" is used for a single explosive device; for example, a single weapon was detonated over Hiroshima, while a large bomber may carry several weapons (bombs and short-range missiles), and a multiple-warhead missile can deliver several weapons against hostile targets. The term "weapon system" embraces the weapon and the various components required for its operation, such as the missile, bomber, or submarine, their crews, maintenance equipment, electronic devices, and so forth. The term is not precise unless specific parameters are established. Basic characteristics of various weapons will be found in the Appendices.

Mr. Polmar has devoted most of his career to the study of US and Soviet military-naval history, strategy, and technology. Since 1967, he has been Editor of the United States sections of the annual *Jane's Fighting Ships*, the "bible of the world navies;" and beginning in 1975, he has been Editor of Jane's *Combat Aircraft Directory*. He served as an executive of the analytical research firm of Lulejian & Associates, Inc., from 1970 to 1975, directing and participating in several studies of military strategy, operations, technology, and intelligence. From 1967 to 1970, he was with the Northrup Corporation, engaged in support of US Navy advanced undersea programs; and before that, he served for four years as Assistant Editor of the authoritative Naval Institute *Proceedings*. Mr. Polmar has written several books, as well as numerous articles on military-naval subjects for American and foreign newspapers, magazines, and encyclopeadias.

Frank R. Barnett, *President*
National Strategy Information Center, Inc.

October 1975

Glossary of Terms

ABM	Anti-Ballistic Missile
ABRES	Advanced Ballistic Reentry System
ALBM	Air-Launched Ballistic Missile
ALCM	Air-Launched Cruise Missile
AMSA	Advanced Manned Strategic Aircraft (now B-1 bomber)
ARPA	(Defense) Advanced Research Project Agency (subsequently DARPA)
ASW	Anti-Submarine Warfare
BMD	Ballistic Missile Defense
BMS	Ballistic Missile Ship
Bus	See PBV
CEP	Circular Error Probable (indicator of weapon accuracy; it is the radius of a circle within which half of the warheads are expected to fall)
FOBS	Fractional Orbital Bombardment System
ICBM	Intercontinental Ballistic Missile (approximately 3,000- to 8,000-nautical mile range)
IRBM	Intermediate-Range Ballistic Missile (approximately 1,500- to 3,000-nautical mile range)
KT	Kiloton (equivalent of 1,000 tons of TNT)
LRA	Long-Range Aviation (Soviet *Aviatsiya Dalnovo Deistviya*)
MaRV	Maneuvering Reentry Vehicle
MIRV	Multiple Independently-targeted Reentry Vehicle
MOBS	Multiple Orbital Bombardment System
MRBM	Medium-Range Ballistic Missile (approximately 600- to 1,500-nautical mile range)
MRV	Multiple Reentry Vehicle
MSBS	*Mer-Sol Balistique Stratégique*
MT	Megaton (equivalent of 1,000,000 tons of TNT)
M-X	Advanced US ICBM
NASA	National Aeronautics and Space Administration

PBV   Post-Boost Vehicle (vehicle that carries multiple reentry vehicles; generally known as "bus")

PVO   Air Defense Forces (Soviet *Protivo-vozdushnoi Oborony Strany*)

RV   Reentry Vehicle

SABMIS   Sea-based Ballistic Missile Intercept System

SAC   Strategic Air Command (US)

SALT   Strategic Arms Limitation Talks

SAM   Surface-to-Air Missile

SIOP   Single Integrated Operational Plan

SLBM   Submarine-Launched Ballistic Missile

SLCM   Submarine-Launched Cruise Missile

SLMS   Ship-Launched Missile System

SRAM   Short-Range Attack Missile

SRF   Strategic Rocket Forces (Soviet *Raketnyye Voyska Strategicheskogo Naznacheniya*)

SSB   Ballistic Missile Submarine

SSBN   Ballistic Missile Submarine (nuclear)

SSBS   *Sol-Sol Balistique Stratégique*

SSG   Guided Missile Submarine

SSGN   Guided Missile Submarine (nuclear)

ULMS   Underwater Long-range Missile System (Trident)

1

An Evolutionary Process

The stillness of the New Mexico desert was torn asunder at 5:30 a.m. on the morning of July 16, 1945, when man exploded the first atomic bomb. Less than a month later, B-29 bombers of the US Army Air Forces released the second and third nuclear weapons over Nagasaki and Hiroshima, destroying both Japanese cities. Another bomb was available, and still more were in production.[1]

This was the beginning of the "atomic age."

Now, three decades later, nuclear and thermonuclear weapons and their delivery systems have become the benchmark of national military power. Indeed, we can define a "superpower" as a nation that could be the victim of a surprise, first-strike attack by any other nation and still inflict massive retaliatory destruction on the aggressor. "Massive destruction" in this context is, as a minimum, destroying a nation's ability to function as a viable, modern society. The Department of Defense in 1970 estimated that the loss of at least 25 percent of the population and 50 percent of the industrial capacity of the Soviet

---

[1] The number of nuclear weapons produced by the US has never been made public. In December 1945, physicist J. Robert Oppenheimer stated that it would take about nine monhs to provide 50 atomic bombs. In retrospect, that estimate appears to have been overoptimistic.

This was Hiroshima after suffering history's first atomic bomb attack. Destruction was almost total because of the light building materials used by the Japanese, the absence of an effective civil defense program, and the lack of warning. Note the still-standing concrete structures. (*US Air Force*)

Union would destroy that nation's ability to function as a modern society.

At this moment, thousands of land- and submarine-based missiles, and hundreds of bombers armed with these weapons of mass destruction, are numbered among the arsenals of the United States, Soviet Union, Britain, France, and the People's Republic of China, while India has also demonstrated the ability to produce such weapons. The past three decades have seen the US strategic position decline from one of absolute monopoly in nuclear weapons, first to a posture of overwhelming superiority, and then to the situation in the early 1970s, when the USSR achieved "parity" or "comparability" with the United States in certain measurements of nuclear striking power, and superiority in others. As this decline took place in the strategic position of the United States *vis-à-vis* the Soviet Union, US strategy changed. At the end of World War II, the defeated Axis nations and many of the victorious allied countries were devastated, their economies and industrial capability unable to support even a peacetime society. In terms of war-fighting capability, the USSR possessed a large and well-armed ground force that could easily have overrun Western Europe, or possibly even China; but the USSR was unable to sustain such a force because of catastrophic conditions in the homeland, nor did it have a long-range air or naval capability to support an aggressive national strategy.

The prevalent strategic view in the Truman phase of the "atomic age" (1945-53) was that long-range bombers carrying nuclear weapons against enemy cities or military forces could defeat any nation or force hostile to the United States and its interests. In this environment, the US Air Force was established as a separate service, and the Army and Navy were reduced to essentially "token" forces. These small ground and naval services would be required in future conflicts primarily to provide certain occupation and logistic forces to support the primary weapon: the long-range bomber.

On June 25, 1950, ground and air forces of Communist North Korea crossed the border into South Korea in an all-out assault to gain control over all of the Korean Peninsula. The perceived US strategy was articulated by one Air Force officer who, when told that US

"Little Boy" and "Fat Man" were the nuclear weapons exploded over Hiroshima and Nagasaki. "Little Boy" weighed some 9,000 pounds, was 120 inches long, and 28 inches in diameter; "Fat Man" weighed about 10,000 pounds, was 128 inches long, and 60 inches in diameter. Later weapons are smaller . . . and more powerful. *(US Air Force)*

ground troops were to be committed to the war, is said to have re-marked: "The old man [General MacArthur] must be off his rocker. When the Fifth Air Force gets to work on them, there will not be a North Korean left in North Korea."

Only after three full years of conventional warfare, involving mostly US air, ground, and naval weapons of World War II vintage, was the Korean War finally brought to a conclusion. US forces had achieved their goal of maintaining the independence of South Korea without the employment of "tactical" or "strategic" nuclear weapons. Both uses were considered—tactical, in the sense of direct support to ground operations (against troop concentrations, bridges, and so forth); and strategic, against mainly factories and assembly areas in North Korea and Manchuria. At that time, essentially the same weapons would have been used in both roles because the size and configuration of nuclear explosives limited them to delivery by large aircraft. Although scientists and engineers were already developing small-size and small-yield nuclear weapons, those available to the armed forces in the early 1950s were still large in size and yield. They could be carried only in the large, multi-engine bombers of the Air Force and a few large, carrier-based Navy aircraft (see Chapter 3). Although their prede-cessors had been used to destroy Japanese cities in 1945, they could also be employed against enemy troop concentrations and staging areas, or against specific industrial-military installations.

Subsequently, the Eisenhower-Dulles Administration (1953-61) enunciated the strategy of massive retaliation, according to which an attack against the United States or its allies would be met with massive nuclear srikes. In this period, the ability of the Soviet Union to attack the United States with nuclear weapons consisted of a few long-range Soviet nuclear bombers that would have had to survive an expansive US warning and air defense system, and with an active US civil de-fense program also in existence.

The shift in Soviet strategy to wars of national liberation and other less direct offensive actions in the 1960s led to a corresponding change in US strategy during the Kennedy-Johnson period (1961-69) to what was called "strategic deterrence." A direct Soviet attack against the United States, and possibly against the NATO countries, would be countered by a US nuclear strike. But conventional military forces would be developed to counter Soviet or other hostile actions at a lower level of conflict. The ten-year Vietnam War exemplified this strategy, with more than half a million US troops fighting what some historians and other analysts have described as a "holding action," and with the national leadership clearly stating that tactical nuclear weapons—available in large numbers—would not be employed.

By the beginning of the Nixon Administration (1969), it was evident that the Soviet Union had embarked on a strategic weapons build-up to attain at least equality with the nuclear arsenal of the United States.[2] At the same time, the cost of the Vietnam War in terms of dollars, popular support, and to some extent even public interest in military matters, had brought about reductions in US strategic defensive forces and a reduced rate of development in new offensive weapons. Then, with the 1972 signing of the first agreement of the Strategic Arms Limitation Talks (SALT I) between the United States and the Soviet Union, the US leadership accepted Soviet superiority in several strategic offensive and defensive systems. Moreover, US leadership in certain other areas, especially multiple warheads for missiles and submarine-launched missiles, appeared to be temporary in view of ongoing Soviet programs.

US-USSR STRATEGIC WEAPONS LIMITATIONS
1972 AGREEMENT

	United States	Soviet Union
Large ICBMs	54	313
Light ICBMs	1,000	1,305
Submarine-Launched Ballistic Missiles (SLBM)	710	950
Strategic Missile Submarines	44	62

(The above are the maximum allowable totals in each category. To reach the submarine missile limit, the United States would have to give up the 54 large Titan ICBMs; while to reach their submarine missile limit, the Soviets would have to give up ap-

---

[2] See Appendix A for ten-year trends in US-USSR strategic weapons forces.

proximately 209 older light missiles of the SS-7 Saddler and SS-8 Sasin types, and 27 missiles in Hotel-class submarines.)

Less explicit than Soviet "parity" or "comparability," three other factors have become evident in the strategic arms "race": (1) Soviet strategic arms development has been both independent and responsive with regard to US actions, but has not copied US developments; (2) the Soviet Union has the capability of matching or exceeding the quantity and, on a longer-term basis, the quality of US strategic forces; and (3) with the current strategic "balance," the possible use of highly selective strategic weapons or tactical nuclear weapons probably is increasing.

With respect to Soviet strategic arms development, certain Soviet weapons appear to have been developed in response to US programs. For example, many Soviet political and military leaders have implied that the massive US strategic bomber deployments of the late 1940s and 1950s could not be matched by Soviet bomber efforts because of technological limitations and geography (the Soviets did not have overseas bomber bases such as were then available to the United States). Accordingly, the Soviet government responded with an emphasis on intercontinental missiles, leading to US fears of a "missile gap" in favor of the USSR during the late 1950s. At the same time, certain Soviet weapon developments, such as the FOBS (Fractional Orbital Bombardment System), appear to be independent of specific existing or planned US weapon capabilities.

The second point—concerning the Soviet ability to match US weapon developments both quantitatively and qualitatively—is evident in the numbers of ICBMs and submarine missiles produced and deployed by the USSR, and by such sophisticated systems as the Soviet satellite intercept weapon, certain Soviet command and control programs, anti-ship missiles, and the multiple warheads associated with the latest generation of Soviet ICBMs.

New Strategic Initiatives

The potential use of selective nuclear weapons in a US-Soviet exchange has long been possible on a tactical basis on land, especially in Europe, and at sea. With respect to a limited nuclear war at sea, the only US ships with nuclear anti-ship weapons are aircraft carriers; at this writing, there were 14 such ships in the active fleet, with the carrier force scheduled to decline to 12 by the late 1970s. On the Soviet side, the Soviet Navy has a large inventory of land-based bombers, large surface warships, small coastal craft, and submarines armed with nuclear anti-ship missiles. There is increasing evidence that certain Soviet submarines armed with ballistic missiles may have an anti-ship (that is, tactical) role instead of a strategic mission.

While nuclear warheads capable of destroying highly selective targets have long been available on a tactical basis, strategic weapons generally are in the multi-kiloton or megaton size. Thus, a strategic bomber delivering a weapon of only 50 kilotons (three times the size of the bomb dropped on Hiroshima) against a specific military or industrial target in an urban area could devastate an entire city. Secretary of Defense James R. Schlesinger began proposing the development of more selective strategic weapons shortly after taking office in mid-1973. With reference to then-existing US strategic weapons doctrine and available weapons, Dr. Schlesinger explained:

> The doctrine as it has been understood in the past . . . does not give us deterrence across the entire spectrum of risk . . . If we have that deterrent across the entire spectrum of risk, we are not going to have war. If we don't have the deterrent across the entire spectrum of risk, then somebody may be tempted through a miscalculation to do something that could escalate into nuclear war.

In testimony before a Senate subcommittee on March 4, 1974, he also stated:

> I must add that for deterrence, one has got to have an implementable threat. If one says that a deterrent is based upon a nonimplementable threat, such as both sides going after each other's cities, what one is saying is that the deterrent is logically unsound.

Proper responsive capabilities in the era of US-Soviet strategic weapons "parity" or "comparability" must, in the opinion of Dr.

Schlesinger, include more selective weapons in order to provide more selective deterrent responsives, such as the ability to destroy part of an opponent's petrochemical industry with a minimum of indication that a wide-scale nuclear attack is under way, and without inflicting major collateral damage on civilians, other industries, or military installations.

In this context, the threat of massive retaliation by the United States or Soviet Union against an aggressor—large or small—has failed too often to inhibit civil wars, limited wars, and wars of national liberation during the past three decades. Moreover, the proliferation of nuclear weapons will increase in future years, infinitely complicating an already complex problem.

2

United States Monopoly

The mass destruction resulting from the first use of nuclear weapons by the United States in 1945 convinced political and military leaders throughout the world that these weapons could have a decisive role in the postwar world. Only one bomber carrying a nuclear weapon—if it could reach its target—would inflict the same damage that previously required thousands of bomber sorties.[3] Nuclear weapons appeared at last to validate the words of airpower advocate Giulio Douhet, written more than two decades earlier:[4]

> The complete destruction of the objective has moral and material effects, the repercussions of which may be tremendous. To give us some idea of the extent of these repercussions, we need only envision what would go on among the civilian population of congested cities once the enemy announced that he would bomb such centers relentlessly, making no distinction between military and nonmilitary objectives.

The beginning of the atomic age was dominated by the fact that only the United States had nuclear weapons and the means to deliver them. The initial delivery method was by four-engine B-29 bombers,

---

[3] The Nagasaki bomb was a 20-kiloton weapon having the equivalent explosive power of 20,000 tons of TNT, or the payload of 4,000 B-29 sorties flown from the Mariana Islands to Tokyo. The Hiroshima-type bomb had a yield of approximately 14 kilotons.
[4] General Giulio Douhet, *The Command of the Air* (originally published in Italian in 1921; translated and published in English in 1942).

The Boeing B-29 Superfortress was the first nuclear delivery aircraft. B-29s comprised the majority of the US strategic bombing force through 1952. The Boeing B-50 was an extensively improved derivative of the B-29, with the same general appearance. (*US Air Force*)

the only delivery platform that could carry such heavy weapons (over five tons for the early bombs) to targets more than a thousand miles from friendly bases. Thus, the initial responsibility for strategic warfare within the US armed forces fell within the province of the Army Air Forces (after 1947, the US Air Force).

During the late 1940s, several improved bomber aircraft were introduced into the US strategic arsenal. First came the B-50, an improved version of the piston-engine B-29, and then the long-range B-36, a piston-engine giant that could, under ideal conditions, fly a round-trip of 10,000 miles with a single early nuclear weapon. Even more significant, production of the B-47, a sleek jet bomber of medium range, was initiated in 1947.

A large force of nuclear-capable B-29, B-50, and B-36 bombers was in service by 1950, and US perceptions of this striking power were considerable. In May 1947, for example, a force of 101 B-29s flew over New York City in a "maximum mission effort" to demonstrate the striking power of the US nuclear arsenal. This was one third of current US strategic bomber strength; another 30 B-29s planned for the mission remained at their bases because of maintenance and supply problems. In a comparably impressive demonstration, a single B-50 flew around the world in March 1949 without landing, being refueled four times in flight by KB-29 tanker aircraft. These flights, as well as overseas flights by small detachments of B-29s, were intended for training as well as to demonstrate the capabilities of the Strategic Air Command (SAC), which operated the US strategic bombers.

The first confrontation with the Soviet Union in which SAC was directed to prepare for a nuclear strike was the Berlin crisis of June 1948, when the Soviets interdicted Allied ground and canal transit to the city. One B-29 squadron was already in West Germany on a training flight; and a short time later, additional B-29 squadrons were flown into West German and British air bases. Some 90 B-29s were forward-based in Europe during the crisis period.

According to US Air Force histories, however, the B-29s dispatched to Europe in 1948 were not capable of carrying atomic bombs. There were in SAC at the time only 32 B-29s modified to deliver nuclear weapons. All of them were assigned to the 509th Bomb Group, which was not deployed to Britain until the Summer of 1949. (Nonnuclear components of atomic bombs were not sent to Britain until 1950, and the nuclear components apparently were not stored in Britain until the mid-1950s.) Had the decision been made to strike the Soviet Union or East Germany with nuclear weapons, several hours would have been required to assemble the bombs, and several more to load and ready the aircraft at bases in the eastern United States. The B-29s would then have had to stage through bases in Britain to be refuelled before going on to their targets. This was a ponderous process, but still the world's only nuclear strike capability.

Airlift rather than atomic bombs became the allied strategy for the "Battle of Berlin." Consideration of US nuclear strike options did, however, point up a number of limitations in SAC capabilities, among them: (1) the limited ranges of aircraft, (2) the inability to store nuclear weapons overseas (even in England), and (3) the lack of ready overseas bases.

Jet Bombers

In 1951, the capability of SAC was improved when the first large B-36s became operational (ten years after contract and three years after first delivery) and the first jet-propelled B-47s were being delivered. The B-36s were big and slow (440 m.p.h. maximum), but could reach the Soviet Union from US bases without in-flight refueling. The B-47 could accelerate to 630 m.p.h. carrying a nuclear weapon, but lacked the range to reach the Soviet Union from bases in the United States. Accordingly, several SAC bases were established in Britain and Morocco in 1950-51, and large numbers of KC-97 tanker aircraft were procured to provide the B-47s with in-flight refueling.

The B-36 was a large airplane (almost 360,000 pounds gross for the D model) powered by six piston engines supplemented by four jet engines in wing pods. Its size and cost made it the most-publicized bomber of the immediate postwar era. Still, its development was predictable, inasmuch as the Air Force continually sought larger bombers that could lift a greater payload of bombs and fuel.

On the other hand, the sleek B-47 was, in the words of Bill Gunston, a leading aviation historian, "a design so advanced technically as to appear genuinely futuristic." The B-47 pushed the US Air Force into the jet bomber age. Designed by the Boeing Aircraft Company, which had produced the famed B-17 and B-29 bombers, the aircraft was one of several designs considered at the end of World War II for the initial generation of jet-propelled bombers. After studying a number of configurations, Boeing engineers took advantage of German research into swept-back wings to produce the final B-47 concept. The pilot and copilot sat in tandem in the narrow fuselage, with a navigator/bombardier in the nose, a total of three men compared to ten for the B-17 and 11 for the B-29, both smaller aircraft. Space and weight were instead allocated to fuel, with the B-47 carrying almost ten times the B-17's capacity and close to three times that of the B-29. The distinctive swept wings of the B-47 carried six jet engines in a twin and single pod on each side. They could push the B-47E to 606 m.p.h. (Mach 0.84 at 16,300 feet), and the plane could carry two nuclear weapons to a combat radius of over 1,600 miles, and farther with in-flight refueling.

B-47s began joining SAC squadrons in 1951, with the ultimate B-47E version making its first flight in 1953. B-47 production totaled 2,060 aircraft, including several hundred EB-47 electronic warfare and RB-47 reconnaissance variants. The B-47 was the most numerous aircraft in SAC during the early 1960s, and was produced in greater numbers than any jet-propelled bomber except possibly the Soviet Tu-16 Badger. In quantity and quality, the B-47 was a milestone in the development of strategic bombers and gave the United States a potent nuclear strike capability.

The Soviets, ever defensively oriented and fully aware of US reliance on nuclear strike aircraft, in the same period revealed a 500-m.p.h. jet fighter-interceptor that could operate at altitudes up to 50,000 feet. This was the MiG-15, a swept-wing fighter that could make bombing missions by the B-36s and B-47s, which flew at lower altitudes, extremely hazardous. Beginning in 1947, some 15,000 to

Sleek and fast, the Boeing B-47 Stratojet was the first jet-propelled "strategic" bomber to be used in large numbers by the United States. Although limited in range, in-flight refueling and overseas bases—plus one-way missions against some targets—made the B-47 an effective strategic bomber. (US Air Force)

The Convair B-36 was big and controversial. It was initially designed and ordered in late 1941. When it became operational a decade later, the B-36 was vulnerable to contemporary piston and jet-propelled fighter aircraft. (*General Dynamics*)

18,000 Mig-15s were built, more than twice the number of F-86 Sabres (which was the most numerous Western jet fighter design) produced.

This massive deployment of interceptor aircraft—which continues today—was part of the Soviet defensive attitude born of numerous invasions of what is now the territorial extent of the USSR. In this century, Russia has been invaded twice by Germany; US, British, French, and Japanese troops landed in Russia and Siberia to fight the Bolsheviks during the latter stages of World War I; and there remains (in the Soviet view, at least) the threat of assault from China in the east and NATO forces in the west. During the post-World War II period, the threats perceived by the Soviets—and which have perpetuated this defensive attitude—have included US and NATO ground forces, bombers, and missiles, and US naval forces.

In the immediate postwar era, the US Navy was without a "strategic" mission. The Navy had emerged from World War II as the unquestioned ruler of the seas. No nation, friend or late foe, had any warships capable of seriously interfering with US use of the sea. The "potential" enemy, the Soviet Union, had neither a fleet nor a reason to use the sea. Not until Korea could the US Navy demonstrate that it still was needed in the atomic age, albeit in support and projection missions (rather than for control of the sea). If future national strategy was to be based on nuclear weapons, those in existence were too large for carrier-based planes, let alone for long-range naval guns, the largest of which was only able to shoot a projectile 16 inches in diameter some 23 miles.

In searching for a role in the nuclear era, the Navy sought the means to deliver nuclear weapons against the Soviet Union or other future enemies. Shipboard and submarine test-launchings were conducted with captured German V-2 rockets and V-1 jet-propelled missiles. But these efforts yielded no practical result until the mid-1950s. More immediately, experiments were undertaken with the P2V Neptune, a twin-engine, long-range patrol/reconnaissance bomber.[5] P2V Neptunes were used in test launches from carrier flight

---

[5] A P2V Neptune held the world's aircraft distance record from 1946 until 1962, having flown a distance of 11,236 miles from Perth, Australia, to Columbus, Ohio. Also, an Army Air

decks, and their bomb-bays were modified to accommodate nuclear weapons. During a series of tests in 1948-49, one or two P2V Neptunes would be loaded aboard one of the Navy's three large carriers of the *Midway* class at dockside.[6] Then, the ship would steam out to sea and launch the aircraft. After taking off, the Neptunes would fly to a simulated target, pretend to release a nuclear weapon, and then return to a land base. In time of war, the crew would either bail out after releasing the weapon or, if it could be coordinated, the plane would fly out to sea and ditch near a waiting US submarine. This one-way bombing mission was also accepted by the US Air Force for reaching certain Soviet targets in central Asia. They were not officially suicide missions. The crews were instructed to reach a neutral nation or, if necessary, bail out over a remote area of the USSR and await the end of the war (a matter of days, at most).

As previously noted, the Korean War, which began in June 1950, shattered the illusions of the nuclear-capable bomber as the final arbiter of modern war. As late as October 19, 1949, General Omar N. Bradley, Chairman of the US Joint Chiefs of Staff, had addressed the question of conventional-versus-strategic actions in these words:

> I am wondering whether we shall ever have another large-scale amphibious operation. Frankly, the atomic bomb, properly de-livered, almost precludes such a possibility.

The Korean War nevertheless included several amphibious landings. (The invasion force at the Inchon landing consisted of a US Marine division, an Army infantry division, most of a Marine aircraft wing, plus supporting troops, all carried and supported by an armada of over 230 ships).

During the three years of war on the Peninsula, the theater com-mander, General Douglas MacArthur, asked that nuclear weapons be employed to halt the masses of Chinese "volunteers" that entered

---

Forces B-29 flew nonstop from Honolulu over the North Pole to Cairo, Egypt, a distance of 9,500 miles. But neither of these flights had any strategic significance, except for testing flight crew endurance, because the planes carried no bombload, and had no schedule, speed, or altitude demands.

[6] The three *Midway*-class aircraft carriers, completed in 1945-47, were the largest warships built during the World War II era except for the two Japanese battleships and one carrier of the *Yamato* class. The *Midway*-class ships displaced 55,000 tons full load, were 986 feet long, and could operate 137 piston-engine carrier aircraft.

North Korea in the winter of 1950-51. President Truman (and other US leaders) were against using nuclear weapons. There was a fear in Washington that American use of nuclear weapons would widen the war, possibly bringing Soviet forces directly into the conflict or precipitating Soviet action in Europe. Other factors included the second use of nuclear weapons against an Asian people, the credibility of the war as a United Nations action if a weapon that only the United States possessed were employed, the difficulty of determining targets that warranted the devastation of nuclear weapons, and the possibly limited number of nuclear weapons in the US arsenal. Reportedly, General MacArthur argued for employing between 30 and 50 bombs. This may have been a significant portion of the nuclear weapons available at the time.

During the Korean War, US striking power in Europe was increased against fear that Korea was merely a Communist diversion in Asia, while the main blow was about to fall in Europe. SAC began rotational training flights of squadrons to overseas bases in order to provide forward deployments of bombers. Most of these flights were sent to Britain, but SAC bombers also operated from bases in French Morocco, Libya, Guam, and Japan. (B-29s participating in the Korean War flew from bases in Japan and Okinawa.)

By this time, the US Navy was ready to make an initial contribution to the nation's nuclear strike capability. In February 1951—eight months after the Korean War began—six of the new AJ-1 Savage (piston) and three P2V-3C Neptune (piston) bombers flew across the Atlantic to Port Lyautey, Morocco. Beginning in March 1951, the Savages periodically flew from two of the large *Midway*-class carriers that were then operating in the Mediterranean.

Both of the aircraft carriers had nuclear weapons on board, having been the first ships modified for handling atomic bombs. The Savages could operate from carriers; but the larger Neptunes had to remain ashore because they required dockside loading by large cranes. Thus, if nuclear war appeared "imminent," the Savages would land on the carriers, refuel, load nuclear weapons, and take off when the carriers came within range (1,600 miles on a one-way trip) of Soviet targets. The bombs were assembled aboard the carriers in special, highly

The North American AJ Savage was the first carrier-based aircraft capable of delivering nuclear weapons. Propelled by two piston engines with a jet booster, the Savage took up a lot of space. Here 11 Savages fill the forward flight deck of the *Coral Sea*. (*US Navy*)

restricted spaces by large numbers of technicians who required about 24 hours to put the bombs together. Still, the aircraft carriers were sovereign US territory, fully independent of the complex considerations involved in a nuclear-armed aircraft taking off from a land base on foreign soil.

Subsequently, additional aircraft carriers, including the smaller *Essex*-class ships, were fitted to handle nuclear weapons. The AJ Savage and, later, A3D Skywarrior (jet) attack planes were added to their normal air groups, up to a dozen planes on the larger carriers, and four planes on each of the *Essex*-class ships.

The Korean War was not a Communist diversionary tactic, and no US-Soviet confrontation occurred during the conflict. US military planners did consider using atomic bombs in the Far East during the Winter of 1950-51, when Communist Chinese troops threatened to destroy the US ground forces in North Korea, and again in the Spring of 1954, when Communist Viet Minh units surrounded a French ground force at Dienbienphu in Indochina. B-29s or B-50s based on American-controlled Okinawa would have been used to strike Chinese troops massing in Manchuria or entering Korea across the Yalu River. The plan for strikes in Indochina presented more complex problems. Initial proposals involved sending large numbers of B-29s from the Philippines or carrier-based planes to pound Viet Minh positions around Dienbienphu with conventional bombs. As the situation worsened for the French, consideration was given to employing nuclear weapons. The sovereignty of the Philippines prevented loading nuclear weapons at US bases in that island nation. Okinawa and Guam were too far for effective use of the B-50s. On the other hand, at least two of the US Navy's eight aircraft carriers in the western Pacific had nuclear weapons on board, and the squadron of AJ Savages then based in Japan could have been rapidly flown out to the carriers to provide a nuclear strike capability.[7]

For a number of reasons, the US government decided against direct intervention with either conventional or nuclear bombs. The reasons

---

[7] Admiral Arthur D. Radford, at the time Chairman of the US Joint Chiefs of Staff, later informed the author that the carrier-based strike option would have been used if the decision had been made to employ nuclear weapons in Indochina.

were similar to those that led to the decision not to use nuclear weapons in Korea. Dienbienphu fell in May 1954, and the First Indochina War soon came to an end. Thus, US military planners did give consideration to using nuclear weapons on three occasions during the periods of US monopoly and overwhelming superiority in nuclear weapons; the Berlin crisis of 1948, the Korean War, and Dienbienphu.

During those years, the US nuclear strike capability increased from a handful of bombs deliverable by piston-powered B-29s to—by 1955 —some 200 B-36s and over 1,000 B-47s capable of carrying atomic bombs. Added to this force was the Navy's growing carrier-based nuclear strike capability. The Navy had lost out in its effort to construct a huge "supercarrier" in 1949. Secretary of Defense Louis Johnson and, to a lesser extent, General (then President of Columbia University) Eisenhower had the decisive influence on a split Joint Chiefs of Staff on the issue of whether or not to build the ship or alternatively, by implication, to emphasize strategic bombers. The Navy continued to argue for a sea-based nuclear strike capability beyond the few AJ Savages aboard its existing carriers. Navy spokesmen contended that "we cannot safely place reliance on any single weapon or weapon system, but must carry a relatively 'full bag'— must keep them versatile and adaptable to any situation." The words were similar to those that would be used two decades later by the proponents of the socalled TRIAD strategic weapons concept, who were arguing against increased reliance on sea-based strategic weapons.

The Korean War demonstrated that navies and even aircraft carriers were still needed in the atomic age, and a program of large carrier construction was begun, initially at the rate of one supercarrier per year. The first, the USS *Forrestal,* was completed in 1955. The *Forrestal* and later large or "super" carriers further increased US forward-deployed nuclear strike capabilities.

3

United States Superiority

The US monopoly of nuclear weapons ended in August 1949, when the Soviet Union exploded a fission device. This event was a milestone on the Soviet path to becoming a superpower, and set the stage for a world with two superpowers. But it would be several years before the Soviet Union had nuclear weapons in large numbers, or the means to deliver them against the United States.

The first Soviet aircraft capable of carrying an atomic bomb was the Tu-4 Bull.[8] Three US B-29 Superfortresses had landed in Soviet Siberia in 1944 after bombing raids against Manchuria and Japan. These aircraft were copied by the Soviets in remarkable time, and the first Tu-4 Bull flew late in 1946. The aircraft was soon in series production, and some 1,200 Bulls were delivered during the next few years. This was how the *Aviatsiya Dalnovo Deistviya*, or Long-Range Aviation (LRA), obtained a "strategic" bomber. With a bomb-load of five and a half tons, the Bull could fly 3,000 miles at a cruising speed of some 225 m.p.h. This meant that by taking off from bases in northern Russia and Siberia, the planes could reach some targets in the northern United States on a 13-hour, one-way flight. The limited number of Soviet bombers available through the 1950s, the duration of their flight, the system of US radar warning stations that stretched across the Canadian Arctic, and the manned interceptor aircraft of the United States and Canada, reduced the potential effectiveness of a Soviet nuclear strike capability against the United States during the decade of the 1950s.

---

[8] Tu-4 is the Soviet designation; B-names are US-NATO designations of Soviet bomber aircraft.

But this limited Soviet nuclear strike capability, and the subsequent Soviet explosion of a nuclear fusion device, spurred additional US strategic weapons developments. The United States exploded the first nuclear fusion or thermonuclear device—the precursor of the hydrogen bomb—on November 1, 1952; the Soviets dramatically followed this achievement less than a year later with their first thermonuclear detonation.

Mastery of fusion technology would have farreaching implications in the arithmetic of nuclear arms. The significance of the thermonuclear or hydrogen bomb lies in the enormous energy-releasing efficiency of fusion as compared with fission. Whereas fission weapons were measured in terms of kilotons (KT), or *thousands* of tons of TNT equivalency, fusion weapons could be discussed only in terms of megatons (MT), or *millions* of tons of TNT equivalent. A one-megaton thermonuclear warhead possesses about 50 times the explosive power of the A-bombs used at Nagasaki, but weighs only half as much and is more compact.[9] This meant that when H-bombs became available in the mid-1950s, one large bomber could deliver four weapons with a combined megatonnage equivalent to three hundred bombs of the size dropped on Japan.[10]

The advent of smaller fission and fusion weapons led to the development of US Air Force and Navy fighter/attack-type aircraft that could deliver "tactical" nuclear weapons. In the Air Force, these new nuclear-capable aircraft began with the F-100 Super Sabre "fighter," while the Navy's first new nuclear plane was the diminutive (11-ton gross weight) A4D Skyhawk. Although these fighter/attack aircraft were considered as "tactical" in US military semantics, an F-100 based in West Germany or an A4D aboard an aircraft carrier in the eastern Mediterranean could deliver a nuclear weapon against cities in the USSR, thus blurring efforts to make clear distinctions between tactical and strategic nuclear delivery systems.

Possibly more significant on a long-term basis, the advent of small nuclear warheads meant that the delivery of weapons of mass destruc-

---

[9] One megaton (MT) is the explosive equivalent of one million tons of TNT, or one thousand kilotons (KT).
[10] Based on estimates that a US B-52 bomber can carry four Mk 28 weapons of about one and a half megatons in its bomb-bay.

tion would become feasible with unmanned missiles. In the United States, this potential was partially fulfilled with the development and limited deployment of low-altitude, air-breathing "cruise" or guided missiles.[11] This concept was an outgrowth of the German V-1 or "buzz bomb," with the missiles following a preset flight path to a fixed target; the lack of terminal accuracy in these weapons was compensated for by the high destructive force of the nuclear warhead.

These cruise missiles included the Air Force's Matador, with a 600-nautical mile range (which was renamed Mace in later variants, with a range of 1,200 nautical miles in the final Mace-B missile), and Snark, with a 5,000-nautical mile range; and the Navy's submarine-launched Regulus-I missile, with a range of 500 nautical miles.[12] The Matador/Mace missiles were forward-based in Europe and the western Pacific, while the limited number of Snark missiles procured were based briefly at Presque Isle, Maine. The Navy adapted two World War II-built submarines to carry two Regulus missiles each and then built three additional submarines, one of which was nuclear-powered, to carry four or five missiles. With only one or two submarines (four or five missiles) as sea at any given time, however, the Navy's Regulus force added comparatively little megatonnage to the nation's nuclear striking forces.

The development of small nuclear warheads also permitted the US Army to deploy "tactical" nuclear weapons. These included tactical weapons such as the nuclear rounds for 280-mm and 8-inch (203-mm) guns, the Honest John and Redstone battlefield missiles, and atomic demolitions—"mines"—that could be emplaced along probable Soviet routes of advance through West Germany. But Army interest in nuclear weapons transcended battlefield use, and led to the Jupiter Intermediate Range Ballistic Missile (IRBM).[13] This was a true rocket missile, developed, like the Redstone, with the help of Werner Von Braun and other former German missile scientists. The Jupiter, with a range of 1,500 miles, was intended for emplacement in NATO

---

[11] Cruise or guided missiles have a variable, aerodynamic flight characteristic whereas ballistic missiles have essentially a fixed, ballistic trajectory.
[12] All missile ranges are given in nautical miles (1.15 statute miles).
[13] ICBM ranges are defined as 3,000 to 8,000 nautical miles; IRBM ranges as 1,500 to 3,000 miles; and MRBM (Medium Range Ballistic Missile) ranges as 600 to 1,500 miles.

A Convair Atlas ICBM rises off a launching pad. Atlas was the first operational US ICBM. Accuracy was on the order of one mile at its maximum range of some 5,500 miles. *(General Dynamics)*

nations for strikes against the Soviet Union; it was a true strategic weapon. Simultaneously, the US Air Force was also developing an interest in ballistic missiles, and initiated the Thor IRBM (1,500 miles) and the Atlas and Titan Intercontinental Ballistic Missiles (ICBM), with initial ranges of 5,500 and 6,300 miles, respectively. Interservice rivalry soon led to the decision that the Air Force would operate all IRBMs and ICBMs. The first six Atlas ICBMs became operational in 1959 in the United States, while the Thor IRBMs were installed in Great Britain under joint UK-US control, and subsequently the Jupiter IRBMs in Greece and Turkey.

In retrospect, the decision to assign IRBMs to the Air Force, which already was directing development of the longer-range ICBMs, cannot be argued. The IRBM and ICBM mission was the same as their characteristic as a land-based weapon. Although submarine-based strategic missiles have the same mission as IRBMs and ICBMs, the nature of the submarine platform with respect to equipment, operation, training, support, and other considerations have so far appeared to warrant their operation by the Navy, and not the Air Force or a separate strategic missile force. With the reallocation of military missile roles, the Defense Department established the Advanced Research Project Agency (ARPA) on February 7, 1958, to manage US space programs. Under ARPA's auspices, the nation's nonmilitary space programs were pushed forward; and, July 16, 1958, the Congress passed an act leading to establishment of the National Aeronautics and Space Administration (NASA) to manage the nation's nonmilitary space activities.

Emphasis on Bombers

Despite the variety of cruise and ballistic missiles put forward by the US services during the 1950s, primary US attention was focused on strategic bombers. The Navy operated 14 to 16 attack carriers in the post-Korea period, each provided with 50 or more nuclear strike aircraft: up to one squadron of large A3D Skywarrior or a later A3J Vigilante attack aircraft, and two or three squadrons of smaller AD Skyraider and A4D Skyhawk bombers. For a brief period, apparently some carrier fighter aircraft were also equipped to deliver nuclear weapons. During periods of crisis, the carriers in the Mediterranean and western Pacific would off-load some of their fighters and embark additional strike aircraft. For example, in 1960-61 the carrier *Coral Sea* operated in the western Pacific with 83 attack aircraft capable of delivering nuclear weapons (plus three electronic aircraft and one cargo aircraft).

The US Air Force reached a peak strategic bomber strength in 1959 with 1,366 B-47s and 488 B-52s, in addition to 174 RB-47 reconnaissance aircraft, which were serviced by over 1,000 KC-97 and KC-135 tanker aircraft. These SAC bombers were the mainstay of US strategic forces, and the nation's available cruise and ballistic missiles and carrier-based bombers paled in comparisons of numbers and megatonnage. For example, the six Atlas-D missiles operational at the end of 1959 could each lift an estimated three-megaton warhead, which was only half the megatonnage that a single B-52 could deliver carrying bombs and short-range nuclear attack missiles.

Through 1957, US production lines produced 2,040 B-47s. These planes, in the strike configuration, could deliver one to two nuclear weapons and had a maximum range of 4,000 miles. Based overseas and requiring in-flight refueling, they could reach Soviet targets and then either fly on to neutral territory or return to base. Beginning in June 1955, the Strategic Air Command received the larger, eight-jet B-52. This aircraft, which first flew in 1952, would become the "ultimate" strategic bomber produced in quantity by the United States. The B-52 could carry four H-bombs some 5,000 miles, hit a target, and return to base without refueling. After the loss of a U-2 reconnaissance aircraft on May 1, 1960, however, Soviet missiles forced low-level flight "profiles" which considerably reduced this distance. Maximum speed of this eight-engine giant is 600 m.p.h. B-52 production ran to 699 aircraft when deliveries stopped late in 1962.

Two subsequent strategic bomber programs were initiated in the 1950s, the B-58 Hustler and B-70 Valkyrie. The B-58, which flew in 1956, was a "small" aircraft (160,000 pounds gross compared to 488,000 pounds for the later model B-52s) designed to streak over targets at twice the speed of sound. A sleek-looking plane with four jet pods slung under a delta wing, the B-58 had a limited range, and

The B-52H was the ultimate configuration of the Boeing Stratofortress. This large, eight-jet bomber has an intercontinental range and comparatively large weapons payload carried internally and on wing pylons. Delivered to the Strategic Air Command between 1955 and 1962, the B-52 will remain in service into the 1980s. The B-52 was employed in a conventional bombing role in the Vietnam War. Up to 60,000 pounds of bombs could be carried in the internal weapons bay and on wing pylons. The aircraft can also be used for laying sea mines; and the concept of employing B-52s in the anti-ship role with Navy-developed Harpoon missiles is under consideration. (Boeing)

only 104 aircraft were built, including some configured as TB-58 trainers. The B-70 program was essentially stillborn. This aircraft, which was to have been the successor to the B-52, was a giant (500,000 pounds gross) six-jet bomber with intercontinental ranges and a service altitude of over 70,000 feet. Top speed was to be more than three times the speed of sound (over 2,000-m.p.h.). The B-70 aircraft was cancelled in 1961 by the incoming Kennedy Administration, which preferred to stress the development of strategic missiles as against bombers, citing the B-70 as being "unnecessary and economically unjustifiable." In addition, the high-flying B-70 would be vulnerable to the advanced missiles being deployed by the Soviets. Only three XB-70 aircraft were produced for research purposes.

Still another factor in the demise of the B-70 were the increasing bomber defense capabilities of the Soviet Union. US concern for Soviet offensive and defensive capabilities in the late 1950s led to several changes in US strategic force procedures. Soviet air defenses improved to the point that SAC and the Navy were obliged to revise bombing procedures in order to provide for low-level attacks where they would be less vulnerable to Soviet radar detection and interception. This was the period (see Chapter 4) of major Soviet reorganization for defense of the homeland and the development of advanced air defense weapons. The latter included new fighter-interceptor aircraft, ground radar warning and intercept control stations, and the installation of Surface-to-Air Missiles (SAM). A Soviet SAM-2 missile shot down a U-2 reconnaissance aircraft high over Sverdlovsk on May 1, 1960, marking the end of several years of US "spy" flights over the Soviet Union at very high altitudes.

Soviet efforts to develop and deploy advanced air defense weapons, again reflecting the traditional Russian emphasis on defense, required US nuclear strike aircraft to shift plans from high-level attacks to low-level strikes. This tactic could reduce the probability of detection and interception, but also would greatly increase aircraft fuel consumption and increase the stress placed on the aircraft structure. In 1958, SAC also began an "airborne alert" on a test basis, always keeping a few nuclear-armed aircraft in flight to reduce their vulnerability to attack while on the ground and to reduce flight time to targets. The SAC Commander-in-Chief, General Thomas S. Power, told Congress that:

We in the Strategic Air Command have developed a system known as airborne alert, where we maintain airplanes in the air 24 hours a day, loaded with bombs, on station, ready to go to the target . . . I feel strongly that we must get on with this airborne alert . . . We must impress Mr. Khrushchev that we have it, and that he cannot strike this country with impunity.

4

Soviet Nuclear Forces

Soviet nuclear forces followed a somewhat different course of development from the United States. At first glance, the Soviets did appear to be following the United States when they copied the B-29 in the Tu-4 Bull aircraft. Then, in the mid-1950s, the West obtained its first look at Soviet jet-era strategic bombers at the annual Moscow air demonstrations.

Probably first on the scene was the Tu-16 Badger, a swept-wing bomber comparable in size, role, and performance to the American B-47. The Badger has only two engines, each developing an estimated 19,180 pounds of thrust, as compared to 7,200 pounds thrust for each of six engines in the B-47E—a manifestation of the Soviet tendency to "build big." First flown in 1952 (five years after the B-47), the Badger began entering service with Soviet Long-Range Aviation in 1954-55. It could carry a bomb load of three and a half tons for a distance of 3,800 miles, meaning that Badgers could reach many cities in the United States on one-way flights from northern Soviet bases. This would be a seven-hour flight at cruise speeds, still long but at the same time more practical than the 13-hour flight of the piston-engine Tu-4 Bulls. Top speed of the Badger is about 620 m.p.h., slightly faster than the B-47.

A short time later, the Tu-20 Bear bomber appeared.[14] First seen in 1955, the Bear is the world's only turbo-prop strategic bomber. It

---

[14] The Soviet military designation for this aircraft is Tu-20. US publications generally identify the Bear as the Tu-95, which is the Tupelov design bureau designation.

The Tu-20 is the world's only turbo-prop strategic bomber. Also known by the Tupolev design bureau designation Tu-95 and the NATO code name Bear, the aircraft has been in first-line Soviet service for more than two decades. Now flown by Long-Range Aviation and Naval Aviation, Bear production apparently continued at least into the early 1970s. This Soviet Navy-flown Bear is being looked over by a US Navy P-4 Phantom fighter. (*US Navy*)

is powered by four large turbo-prop engines mounted on swept wings, each having two counter-rotating propellers. The Bear can reach a maximum speed of 550 m.p.h., and can carry a 12-ton bombload to targets 3,000 to 4,000 miles away and return to base.

Soviet LRA squadrons began receiving Bear bombers in 1956-57, and by the end of the decade, some 150 Bears and well over 1,000 Badgers were in service. (Total production was approximately 300 Bears and 1,500 to 2,000 Badgers, with over 50 of these Bears and 500 Badgers being transferred to the Soviet Navy's air arm.) The combined payload of the LRA Bear and Badger force probably totaled no more than 10,000 megatons, a fraction of the estimated 25,000 to 60,000 megatons carried by the US bombers flown by SAC and the Navy.

Soviet industry produced other strategic bombers in this period, notably the four-jet Mya-4 Bison. But like the Tu-20 Bear, these aircraft were only a limited success in the strategic bombing role because of slow aircraft speed, the long intercontinental flight distances to US targets, and the need to overfly Canada, where warning and intercept installations could be based. Most of the 200 to 300 Bisons produced were rapidly adapted to tanker, photographic, or electronic-reconnaissance roles.

The capabilities of LRA were enhanced in the mid-1950s when strategic cruise missiles were provided for the Bear and Badger aircraft. These missiles permitted the bombers to "stand off" from their targets by 100 miles or more, and launch nuclear-tipped missiles that would be less vulnerable to interception than the larger bombers. The Soviets favored the use of stand-off weapons to a much greater degree than the US Air Force, a technique that would increase the attack potential of less capable planes. The differences in the US and Soviet attitudes toward stand-off weapons possibly relate to differing concepts of strategic bombing as they have evolved since the 1920s. During World War II, the Norden bombsight was developed for use in B-17 and B-24 bombers to strike specific military and industrial installations in an effort, albeit futile in many instances, to avoid collateral civilian damage. The Soviets did not have this tradition of strategic bombing; rather, Soviet emphasis on defense bespoke the

Another sleek-looking and long-serving product of the Tupolev design bureau is the Tu-16 Badger, a twin-jet aircraft that is in wide use with Soviet Long-Range Aviation and Naval Aviation in the bomber, missile strike, reconnaissance, and electronic warfare roles. This Badger-D, with a nose radome, is fitted for reconnaissance and anti-ship missile guidance; most Badgers have glazed noses. (*US Navy*)

need to penetrate intensive anti-bomber defenses, which could be better accomplished by a stand-off missile that presents less of a radar target and has a greater speed than a manned bomber.

More significant than the LRA Bears and Badgers were Soviet strategic missile developments. Whereas US strategic bombers could strike the Soviet Union from bases in Europe, North Africa, Guam, and Okinawa, Soviet A-bombers would have a long polar flight across the Arctic regions and Canada before they could reach the United States. As Party Chairman Khrushchev explained:[15]

> Our potential enemy—our principal, our most dangerous enemy —was so far away from us that we couldn't have reached him with our air force. Only by building up a nuclear missile force could we keep the enemy from unleashing war against us.

Geography, the lack of a strategic bomber "tradition," and possibly a Russian ability to examine alternatives rather than accept "obvious" solutions, led to Soviet emphasis on the development of ICBMs in this period. Under Khrushchev's direction, increased resources were allocated to research and development work based on the German V-2 missile. Finally, on August 3, 1957, an SS-6 ICBM rocketed several thousand miles from its launch pad to impact in Soviet Siberia. In guarded words, the Soviet news agency *Tass* announced that a "super-long-distance, intercontinental multistage ballistic rocket flew at an . . . unprecedented altitude . . . and landed in the target area." Not for another 16 months would an American Atlas ICBM be tested over its full range.

Barely two months after the first Soviet long-range ICBM test, an SS-6 booster missile carried Sputnik 1 into orbit, the earth's first artificial satellite. This satellite weighed 184 pounds, or 166 pounds heavier than the first US satellite, which would not be placed into orbit for another three months. And on November 3, 1957, a month after Sputnik 1, the Soviets launched another satellite, placing the then-phenomenal payload of 1,121 pounds into earth orbit. On board Sputnik 2 was the live dog Layka, instrumented to relay biological

---

[15] N. S. Khrushchev, *Khrushchev Remembers* (Boston: 1970), p. 516.

data to earth on the animal's reaction to weightlessness, radiation, and other environmental changes. The satellite Sputnik 3, which was launched into orbit in May 1958, weighed 2,926 pounds, a size not matched by the United States until 1964. These large Soviet satellite payloads could be traded off in early Soviet ICBMs for greater range or more payload; subsequently, when more efficient nuclear warheads became available, advanced Soviet ICBMs could lift much larger payloads than their American counterparts.

The early Soviet technological developments that led to these ICBM and satellite accomplishments, and the accompanying advances in nuclear and hydrogen warheads, made it clear that the USSR was embarked on a strategic missile effort far superior to that planned by the United States. In February 1956, Soviet Defense chief G. I. Zhukov, addressing the 20th Communist Party Congress in Moscow, had declared that the Soviet armed forces had been "completely transformed" since World War II, and that the USSR already had "diverse atomic and hydrogen weapons, powerful rockets and jet armament of various kinds, including long-range rockets." Although Soviet IRBMs could not reach the United States, such weapons could strike Britain and France. Thus, when Anglo-French forces invaded Egypt in November 1956 in concert with an Israeli assault into the Sinai toward the Suez Canal, the Soviets threatened Britain and France with missile attacks if the invasion were not halted. Even though the Soviet threat came after the Eisenhower Administration had announced its absolute opposition to the Anglo-French assault, the Soviet statement did indicate sufficient confidence to engage in "missile rattling."

The Soviet Navy apparently shared in these early strategic weapon developments. Among the German war material that fell into Soviet hands in 1945 were several submarine-towed containers for V-2 missiles. After being towed underwater to within striking range of an enemy coast, the containers were to be ballasted to the vertical position, the missile fueled and checked out, and then fired against the enemy's coastal cities.

Although none of these V-2 containers is believed to have become operational in the Soviet Navy, the concept of Submarine-Launched Ballistic Missiles (SLBM) was clearly recognized by Soviet "technocrats," and by the early 1950s a major effort was clearly underway to provide the Soviet Navy with an SLBM capability. The first experimental launch of a ballistic missile from a Soviet submarine took place in September 1955. This was four and a half years before the first launchings of US Polaris SLBM test missiles.

During the period 1955-57, seven Soviet diesel submarines were configured with two tubes for the surface launch of the SS-N-4 Sark missile. This weapon had a range of about 300 nautical miles, and could carry a nuclear warhead. These conversions were followed by 23 "Golf" diesel submarines and nine "Hotel" nuclear submarines completed between 1958 and 1962, each of which could fire three of the SS-N-4 Sark missiles.[16] Meanwhile, the first Soviet A-submarine went to sea in 1959, less than five years after the USS *Nautilus*. Although all of these submarines were of limited capability in comparison to later US and Soviet ballistic missile undersea craft, they were a clear indication of the direction of strategic weapons development in the USSR.

Strategic Reorganization

Another aspect of Soviet weapons development and strategy were the reorganizations of the Khrushchev era (from 1953, when he was one of three "coequal" successors to Stalin, to his removal in late 1964). The principal services of the USSR traditionally were the Army and Navy. By the end of World War II, the Soviet Air Forces (plural) were firmly established as a separate, albeit secondary, service. The Soviet leadership long had emphasized defense against air attack, and air defense efforts were formalized about 1954 into a separate service, the *Protivo-vozdushnoi Oborony Strany* (Air Defense of the Country). Known by its abbreviation PVO, the new service controlled Soviet fighter-interceptor aircraft, anti-aircraft guns, surface-to-air missiles, and the related warning and communication activities.

The loss of fighter-interceptors to PVO weakened the position of the Soviet Air Forces, as did the vesting of operational control over

---

[16] Postwar Soviet submarine classes are assigned letter code designations by US-NATO intelligence, with the phonetic names "Golf" and "Hotel" being used for the letter "G" and "H" designations, respectively.

The Soviet Navy took ballistic missiles to sea several years before the US Navy. After converting several diesel submarines to carry SLBMs, Soviet shipyards built 23 Golf-class and nine Hotel-class submarines to carry three short-range SLBMs in their enlarged conning towers. (*US Navy*)

the *Aviatsiya Dalnovo Deistviya* (Long-Range Aviation) and the troop-carrying transport aircraft in the Soviet high command. *Morskaya Aviatsiya* (Naval Aviation) remained under total Navy control. Finally, the Soviet tactical air force, officially known as *Frontovaya Aviatsiya* (Frontal Aviation), often operated under direction of fronts or armies on a tactical basis.

Khrushchev's interest in the development of intercontinental missiles as the prime striking force of the USSR and his modernization of Soviet strategy led to establishment in May 1960 of the *Raketnyye Voyska Strategicheskogo Naznacheniya* (Strategic Rocket Forces) as a separate service. The Rocket Forces were given responsibility for development and operation of all Soviet intermediate and intercontinental-range ballistic missiles. Unlike the US Strategic Air Command, which controls US land-based ICBM and strategic bomber forces, the Soviet Rocket Forces do not control Soviet long-range bombers.

Thus, the USSR has five separate and distinct combat services; in their normal order of listing, they are:

(1) Strategic Rocket Forces
(2) Air Defense Forces
(3) Ground Forces
(4) Air Forces
(5) Navy

The technological advances of the Soviet Union during the latter 1950s did not go unnoticed in the United States. American government and military leaders were faced with two kinds of evidence with respect to Soviet activities. First, there was the verbose bragging of Khrushchev and the "unconfirmed reports" of ominous Soviet military developments. For example, the 1958-59 edition of the annual *Jane's All the World's Aircraft* announced that the Soviets had in operation a six-jet, intercontinental bomber twice as fast as any US bomber then in service. Early in 1959, nuclear experts told Congress that within a year the Soviets would fly a nuclear-powered airplane; a year later, the trade journal *Missiles and Rockets* said that the Soviets were testing a semi-ballistic bomber aircraft with a range of almost 10,000 miles and a maximum speed of almost 14,000 m.p.h.;

and press reports of Soviet ICBM tests into the Pacific gave the missiles considerably more accuracy than US weapons. Even the Soviet Navy was being credited with a nuclear strike capability against the United States. One official estimate declared that Soviet missile submarines could launch a "devastating" attack against the United States "early in the 1960s." The second category of indications were the factual indications of Soviet research and experiments in the strategic weapons field. These included the development of fission and fusion warheads before Western intelligence services had predicted.

Soviet developments—real and imagined—led to Senate air power hearings during the spring of 1956 under the gavel of Senator Stuart Symington, who had served as first Secretary of the Air Force. Senior officers of the Air Force testified that there would be a serious "bomber gap" by the early 1960s unless the United States immediately allocated top priority to long-range bomber development. Then came the Soviet ICBM test flights and space spectaculars of 1957, which gave rise to an even more intensive debate which, by the eve of the national election of 1960, became known as the "missile gap" controversy. Once again, US military leaders appeared before Congressional committees to explain the strategic advantages that were accruing to the Soviets through these tests.

The US government initiated counteractions during the late 1950s. A portion of the Strategic Air Command's bombers were placed on airborne alert; Navy carriers in the Mediterranean and western Pacific kept several nuclear-armed aircraft on their flight decks ready for launching; Thor and Jupiter IRBMs were emplaced in Britain, Italy, and Turkey; and the US long-range ICBM programs were accelerated, as was development of the Navy's submarine-launched Polaris missile system.

Late in 1955, the Navy had been directed to join the Army in the Jupiter IRBM program, with the goal of placing the 60-foot, liquid-fueled 1,500-mile missiles at sea in submarines. This order was a result of concern over rapid Soviet advances in H-bomb development. Two years later, with smaller warheads and solid propellents becoming feasible for missiles, the Navy dropped the Jupiter effort and initiated the Polaris SLBM program. The original Polaris schedules called for the first missile submarine to be ready for sea in 1963. Concern over Soviet developments led to revisions of schedules and a dramatic intensification of effort, with the result that the first Polaris submarine, the USS *George Washington,* went to sea on its first "deterrent patrol" on November 15, 1960. The nuclear-propelled *George Washington* carried 16 Polaris A-1 missiles armed with nuclear warheads which could be launched from underwater to targets 1,200 miles away. There was a similar acceleration in the development of the longer-range A-2 and A-3 variants of the Polaris missile.

Ironically, there was considerable Navy opposition to the Polaris program because of fears that (1) the SLBM effort would compete with the Air Force for strategic missions (and, with memories of the Navy defeat in the 1949 carrier-*versus*-B-36 controversy, there was nothing to be gained from such a dispute), and (2) an accelerated Polaris effort would cost the Navy funds for other programs, especially aircraft carriers. Both fears were justified although, in the long run, the Polaris program would be to the Navy's benefit.[17]

When President Kennedy entered the White House in January 1961, the Navy had two Polaris submarines (32 missiles) at sea and 12 others (192 missiles) under construction or fitting out. He immediately ordered five additional submarines, and requested funds from Congress for another ten, to bring the number of such craft on order to 29. President Kennedy also greatly accelerated US strategic weapons development and deployment, although the numbers of ICBMs, IRBMs, bombers, and SLBMs then in service and on order were already superior to existing Soviet strategic weapons capable of reaching the United States.[18]

---

[17] A comprehensive discussion of these arguments appears in Harvey M. Sapolsky, *The Polaris Systems Development* (Cambridge, Mass.: 1972).

[18] It soon became evident to those who had access to the intelligence data, that a "missile gap" actually existed in favor of the United States, when one considered overall program efforts. In the early 1960s, however, the Soviets were initiating the research and development that would lead to Soviet leadership in several categories of strategic weapons before the decade was over.

A US Polaris missile submarine awaits its "teeth." This unusual photograph shows a Polaris submarine with the 16 missile tubes open; each holds an SLBM some 30 feet long. The US Navy built 41 of these modern missile submarines between 1959 and 1967. In 1967, the Soviet Union completed its first modern (i.e., 16-tube) SLBM submarine. *(US Navy)*

5

Confrontation and Restructuring

The "missile gap" that haunted the United States in the late 1950s failed to materialize during the next decade. Despite Khrushchev's directives and bellicose pronouncements, Soviet management and production capabilities were unable to keep pace with the new weapons technologies.

There also were severe operational and personnel problems. The first Soviet ICBM, the SS-6 Sappwood system,[19] fell short of its range goal and could only reach the United States from launch positions in the northern latitudes, on the Arctic islands of Novaya Zemlya and the Franz Josef groups, and the Arctic mainland at Norilsk and Vorkuta. At those northern latitudes, the climate adversely affected missile reliability and logistics. An advanced Soviet missile engine exploded during a test launch in October 1960, killing the first head of the Strategic Rocket Forces, Marshal Mitrofan Nedelin, and over 300 other observers. This tragedy, as well as other accidents, the problems of training missile officers, and other difficulties of the Soviet strategic weapons programs have been described by General Staff Colonel-turned-Western spy Oleg Penkovskiy, and by Khrushchev himself.[20]

---

[19] Designations and names for Soviet missiles are US-NATO designations; "S" names indicate surface-to-surface weapons. Of late, only the designations are used.
[20] Oleg Penkovskiy, *The Penkovskiy Papers* (New York: 1965). Based primarily on the documents sent to the West by Penkovskiy before his exposure and execution by the Soviet government in 1963. Also see N. S. Khrushchev, *Khrushchev Remembers: The Last Testament* (Boston: 1974).

In an apparent effort to recoup his position in the face of Soviet difficulties and Western alarm, Khrushchev made a surprise move during the Fall of 1962 by sending Medium-Range Ballistic Missiles (MRBM) and nuclear-capable bombers to Communist Cuba. Possibly he expected that these weapons, secretly transported to Cuba in merchant ships, could tip the balance of strategic power to the Soviet side. At the least, they could provide a negotiating tool for Khrushchev.

US intelligence detected the Soviet attempt to introduce offensive weapons into Cuba. The Kennedy Administration decided that this situation was unacceptable, and various options were considered for ending the threat of attack from Cuba. These options included destroying the Soviet missiles and bombers by air attack, which proponents acknowledged could not insure total success and would kill Russians; a combined airborne-seaborne assault on the island, which would have led to prolonged and costly ground combat in the island's towns and mountains; or a naval blockade, camouflaged by the expression "quarantine," to halt the further shipment of offensive weapons. The last option, if unsuccessful, still would permit the execution of one or both of the others. Accordingly, on October 22, 1962, President Kennedy announced a 500-mile barrier around Cuba through which no strategic weapons would be permitted. US strategic striking forces were placed on alert, and the White House announced that a Cuban-based attack against any target in the Western Hemisphere would be considered an attack against the United States by the Soviet Union.

At the time of confrontation, the United States had several times the long-range strategic weapons and deliverable megatonnage available to the Soviet Union. In addition, the US Navy could—and did—deploy a massive force of general purpose ships—aircraft carriers, cruisers, destroyers, and submarines—in the Caribbean, while the Soviets were unable to project a force of surface warships across the Atlantic to the crisis area. Still, it was the US arsenal of strategic weapons, tabulated below, that made the Cuban missile crisis a dramatic example of US military superiority.

US AND SOVIET STRATEGIC WEAPONS (Fall 1962)

United States	Soviet Union (Approximate)
639 B-52 heavy jet bombers	100 Tu-20 Bear and Mya-4 Bison heavy bombers[21]
880 B-47 medium jet bombers[22] 76 B-58 medium jet bombers plus carrier-based strike aircraft	1,350 medium jet bombers
142 Atlas ICBMs 62 Titan-I ICBMs 80 Minuteman-I ICBMs	35 SS-6 Sappwood and SS-7 Saddler ICBMs
60 Thor IRBMs 45 Jupiter IRBMs	
112 Polaris A-1 and A-2 SLBMs in seven nuclear-propelled submarines	

Excluded from the above comparison of strategic weapons are the large IRBM force on Soviet territory that could not reach the United States, while the US Thor and Jupiter IRBMs in Britain, Italy, and Turkey could reach Soviet cities. Similarly, several US Polaris submarines at sea could have fired their weapons against the Soviet Union with only minimal interference from hostile anti-submarine forces. Moreover, the Soviet SLBM force, consisting of about 30 diesel submarines and several nuclear submarines, was not able to deploy rapidly and cross the Atlantic to bring their short-range (350-nautical mile) missiles into the confrontation. In addition, US

---

[21] Additional Mya-4 Bisons served in the reconnaissance and tanker roles.
[22] Additional B-47s served in reconnaissance and electronic warfare roles.

anti-submarine forces were comparatively effective. According to one US admiral: "During the Cuban crisis . . . our ASW forces flushed all (six) Soviet submarines en route to the Caribbean within a matter of a couple of days from the word 'Go.' "

Thus, the United States had strategic superiority. It would be another decade before the Soviet Union could achieve comparable strategic forces. The Soviets withdrew their nuclear-capable missiles and bombers from Cuba. Of course, Cuba remained available as a naval and air base for Soviet "conventional" forces. Apparently as part of the US-Soviet accord, US-controlled Jupiter missiles were removed from Italy and Turkey. The removal was offset by the simultaneous entry of Polaris submarines into the Mediterranean in April 1963.

Khrushchev survived the Cuban missile crisis by exactly two years. His ouster as First Secretary of the Communist Party and Prime Minister in mid-October 1964 was due to a number of factors, among them the Soviet backdown in the Cuban missile confrontation. Even while Khrushchev remained in office, the Kremlin leadership, after some debate, made the decision to increase Soviet strategic weapons both qualitatively and quantitively. Obviously, research and development efforts for these programs had been under way for several years.

The number of SS-7 Saddler ICBMs, which first became operational sometime in 1962, was increased; and in 1963, the SS-8 Sasin ICBM became operational. Both missiles had storable-liquid fuels, a range in excess of 6,000 nautical miles, and carried five-megaton warheads. By the time of Khrushchev's removal late in 1964, an estimated 200 ICBMs were emplaced in the Soviet Union, mostly SS-7 and SS-8 missiles. In this period, too, the Soviets began emplacing missiles in underground silos in an effort to hide them from US overhead (satellite) surveillance, and to increase their survivability in the event of a US preemptive attack.

A succession of new ICBMs entered with the Soviet Strategic Rocket Forces in the latter 1960s. The huge SS-9 Scarp became operational in 1967. It had a greater payload than any other operational ICBM. The SS-9 can deliver a 25-megaton warhead on targets

The massive SS-9 Scarp can carry a larger payload than any other ICBM in the US or Soviet strategic arsenal. The missile, which became operational in 1966, has several variants. One modification can carry a 25-MT warhead for attacking "hard" or protected targets; another carries three warheads; and one model has been tested in both a depressed trajectory and in a fractional orbital (FOBS) mode. Many of the 288 SS-9s originally deployed have been replaced by later large-payload missiles.

6,000 nautical miles away. The giant SS-9 soon was employed in tests of the first Soviet multiple-ICBM warhead, and then with the Fractional Orbital Bombardment System (FOBS). Under the FOBS concept, the missile is fired in a low trajectory in the opposite direction from the target, enters a partial earth orbit, and then strikes the target. This tactic increases the problems of defending a target, increases the range of the weapon, and provides considerably less warning than an ICBM following a high ballistic trajectory. In this configuration, however, the SS-9 has less accuracy and carries a smaller warhead.

Following the SS-9 into service, the Soviets began deploying the SS-11 in 1966 and the SS-13 in 1969. Both of these ICBMs were smaller weapons, the SS-11 having a storable-liquid propellant that could strike targets in the United States with a one-megaton warhead; the SS-13, which introduced solid-fuel propellant to Soviet ICBMs, has a range of some 5,500 nautical miles, and also carries a one-megaton warhead.

Numerical Superiority

By 1970, the Soviet Union had surpassed the United States in numbers of operational ICBMs: over 1,100 Soviet missiles to 1,054 US missiles. Of the former, more than 275 were the large SS-9s. In the mid-1960s, moreover, the Soviet Union initiated a major construction program of strategic missile submarines.

The Soviet Navy had completed nine nuclear (Hotel) and 23 diesel (Golf) submarines, each armed with three SLBMs, between 1958 and 1962. In addition, a few older diesel submarines had been converted to fire two of the early missiles. Their limitations have already been described. In 1968, the Soviet Navy completed the first Yankee-class submarine. This was one year after the US Navy completed the last of 41 nuclear submarines armed with the Polaris missile. The Yankee is a modern nuclear undersea craft, similar in size to the US Polaris, carrying 16 SLBMs. The initial Yankee SS-N-6 missiles have a range of 1,300 nautical miles, and carry a warhead unofficially estimated at one to two megatons. (In comparison, the initial 1,200-nautical mile Polaris A-1 missile was followed to sea in 1962 by the

1,500-nautical mile A-2 variant, and in 1964 by the 2,500-nautical mile A-3 variant.)

By 1970, there were about ten Yankee-class SLBM submarines (160 missiles) at sea, with annual production estimated at eight submarines a year. US defense officials stated that "as production experience is gained, it is possible that the rate of output . . . will increase significantly . . . At current construction rates, the Soviets could have from 35 to 50 of the (Yankee) class submarines by 1974-75" (carrying 560 to 800 missiles).

While building up ICBM and SLBM forces during the latter 1960s, the Soviet leadership maintained the level of heavy bombers in Long-Range Aviation, but gradually reduced the medium bomber strength of LRA. In the early 1970s, US defense officials rated LRA at a strength of 150 Bear and Bison bombers, plus 50 Bisons configured as tankers, and over 700 medium bombers. An increasing number of aircraft in both categories were armed with air-to-surface missiles.[23] The Tu-16 Badgers, in service since 1954-55, were joined in the early 1960s by another medium bomber, the Tu-22 Blinder, an aircraft that can reach a maximum speed of 925 m.p.h. (Mach 1.4 at 40,000 ft.) with two turbo-jet engines rated at a phenomenal 26,000 pounds of thrust each. But, whereas the Badger has an unrefuelled range of 3,800 miles with a nuclear weapon, the Blinder's range is only some 2,800 miles, although this can be extended by in-flight refueling. Together with the increases in Soviet ICBM and SLBM forces, the current LRA medium bomber force of about 550 Badgers and 175 Blinders is probably intended exclusively for operations in the Eurasian theaters (see Chapter 8).

A final consideration in the development of Soviet strategic weapons in this period is the cruise missile submarine. As noted earlier, after World War II the US Navy, using German V-1 pulse-jet rocket tech-

---

[23] From 1960, the AS-3 Kangaroo, with a range of 350 nautical miles; from 1967, the AS-4 Kitchen, with a range of 250 nautical miles; and from 1970, the AS-6, with a range of 300 nautical miles. Under present assumed weapons loadings, US officials estimate that the 150-plane Bear-Bison force can deliver up to 250 nuclear gravity bombs and missiles against the United States in an all-out attack. The number of weapons could be increased severalfold if only nuclear bombs were carried.

nology, developed the Regulus submarine-launched cruise missile. This weapon was pursued as a strategic weapon for use against land targets because of the lack of hostile surface fleets and the need to compete with the US Air Force for strategic missions.

Building on the same German technology (and, like the US armed services, employing German scientists and technicians), by the mid-1950s the Soviets undertook the construction of destroyers and coastal craft armed with anti-ship cruise missiles. Next, several Whiskey-class diesel submarines were converted to fire the large Shaddock SS-N-3 anti-ship missile. This weapon has a high subsonic speed, a maximum range of over 400 nautical miles, and can carry some 2,000 pounds of high explosives or a nuclear warhead in the kiloton range. The initial Whiskey-class conversions carried one or two Shaddocks housed in horizontal cylinders aft of their conning towers. The submarines would surface, the cylinders were elevated, and the missiles fired. These were followed by the "long-bin" Whiskey conversions, which had four angled Shaddock tubes fixed in their conning towers.

After these 13 conversions,[24] the Soviet Navy took delivery of several classes of specially-built Shaddock missile submarines: 16 of the diesel Juliett class, each with four missiles; five Echo-I-class nuclear submarines, each with six missiles; and 27 of the Echo-II-class nuclear submarines armed with eight missiles. Today the Juliett and Echo-II submarines remain in first-line Soviet service, as well as a number of newer submarines armed with shorter-range anti-ship missiles.

Although the Shaddock SS-N-3 missile generally is considered an anti-ship weapon, it can be employed with equal versatility against land targets. Some observers contend that the Shaddock was deployed in submarines to provide missile coverage of the southern United States when Soviet land-based missiles and manned bombers could only reach the northern regions of the country. A US Navy presenta-

---

[24] According to *Jane's Fighting Ships* and other naval publications, the Soviet Navy converted one single-cylinder Whiskey submarine, five twin-cylinder Whiskey submarines, and seven "long-bin" Whiskey submarines. The early ships with exposed missile cylinders were extremely noisy because of their awkward configuration and probably were relegated primarily to test and training roles.

tion to Congress in 1973 noted "we know that [Shaddocks] are tactical cruise missiles. But we also are certain that with a modification, which really involves only the warhead of the missile," the Shaddock could be employed as a strategic weapon. In the same session, Navy officials pointed out that a Shaddock-armed submarine operating 150 nautical miles off the US coast could strike coastal cities and as far inland as Pittsburgh, Atlanta, and Dallas. Shaddock-armed submarines, which have periodically operated in the Caribbean Sea at least since 1970, possess the capability of striking targets in the southern United States. These submarine missiles, with their low flight profile and southerly direction of attack, strain US detection and defense capabilities, and add another dimension to the Soviet strategic weapons threat.

During the latter 1960s, the Soviet strategic weapons forces attained a high rate of deployment, with emphasis on ICBMs and SLBMs, in addition to several of the Shaddock missile submarines possibly being assigned to a strategic strike role. Significantly, the Soviet Union did not improve its long-range bomber force, apparently because of (1) the geographic limitations to direct USSR-to-US bomber strikes, (2) the lack of overseas bases for Soviet bombers and tankers, (3) the lack of a politically strong air force organization to compete for long-range bomber development, and (4) the logic in an approach to weapons development that differed from that of the United States.

US Second-Generation Weapons

As the Soviets reached a high rate of ICBM and SLBM deployments in the late 1960s, the US deployment of new strategic weapon "platforms" ended. The Kennedy Administration, which began in January 1961 in the "missile gap" period, undertook an acceleration of both strategic and conventional warfare programs. Simultaneously, the concept of systems analysis was brought forward to a previously unprecedented degree in an effort to develop the optimum "mix" of strategic forces. The nature of the future strategic mix was discussed in these terms by President Kennedy's Secretary of Defense, Robert S. McNamara:

> The introduction of ballistic missiles is already exerting a major impact on the size, composition, and deployment of the manned bomber force, and this impact will become greater in the years ahead. As the number of . . . ballistic missiles increases, requirements for strategic aircraft will be gradually reduced. Simultaneously, the growing enemy missile capability will make gounded aircraft more vulnerable to sudden attack.

During the early 1960s, the remaining US first-generation ICBMs became operational: the Atlas-E in 1960, the Titan-I in 1962, and the Atlas-F in 1962, all with storable-liquid propellants and capable of reaching the Soviet Union from launching pads in the United States.

These weapons were followed into service by the second-generation missiles, the Minuteman-I and Titan-II. The Minuteman-I (of which there were actually two versions developed simultaneously), had a solid propellant and could deliver a one-megaton warhead against targets 6,300 nautical miles away. The Minuteman was installed in underground launch silos to provide protection against preemptive enemy missile or bomber attacks on the US deterrent force. Whereas the Minuteman was a "light" ICBM, the Titan-II was the largest US ICBM to be developed, weighing almost five times as much as the Minuteman and carrying a warhead of about ten megatons a distance of 6,300 nautical miles.

As the Minuteman and Titan programs got under way, their proponents advocated large deployments to insure numerical superiority over Soviet strategic forces. Proponents talked about force levels up to 2,500 Minuteman ICBMs. Actual planning in the early 1960s provided for 1,200 Minuteman missiles and 120 Titan-II weapons as the second-generation SAC missile force. Although Secretary McNamara favored missiles over bombers, he restricted the numbers of ICBMs deployed to what he considered realistic force levels. In addition, the improved Minuteman-II (first operational in 1966) had increased accuracy over the previous Minuteman missiles.

Accordingly, the eventual force levels were established as 1,000 Minuteman and 54 Titan missiles. At the same time, Secretary McNamara accelerated the phasing out of the earlier strategic missiles.

The Snark long-range cruise missile was discarded in 1961, less than four months after some 30 of these weapons had been declared combat-ready. The exposed Thor IRBMs in Britain, operated jointly by SAC and the Royal Air Force, were discarded in 1963. During the next two years, all of the nation's first-generation ICBMs were phased out: the 30 Atlas-D, 33 Atlas-E, 80 Atlas-F, and 63 Titan-I missiles. These actions led to the stabilization of the ICBM force at 1,000 Minuteman and 60 Titan missiles in the mid-1960s, essentially the number of ICBM "platforms" that would be in the SAC inventory for the next decade. Significant qualitative improvements were made to these weapons and will be discussed in the next chapter.

With respect to manned strategic bombers, the Kennedy Administration began phasing out the entire B-47 medium bomber force. SAC jet bomber strength reached a peak of 1,854 aircraft in late 1959: 488 of the intercontinental B-52s, and the remainder medium-range B-47s. The phaseout of older B-47s actually began in 1959, and was accelerated after the Kennedy Administration took office in January 1960. The Berlin crisis of 1961 and the Cuban crisis of 1962 briefly delayed the B-47 phaseout, and the deliveries of B-52 and B-58 jet bombers also briefly offset the B-47 reductions.

The strike capabilities of the B-52 aircraft were improved beginning in 1961 when the Hound Dog air-to-ground missile and the Quail decoy missile became operational. A B-52 could carry two Hound Dog missiles under each wing. These turbojet missiles have a maximum speed of over Mach 2 and a maximum range of over 500 miles for attacking enemy defenses or heavily defended targets. Each Hound Dog has a warhead of about one-megaton. The Quail decoy, carried in the rear bomb-bay of a B-52, is also turbojet-powered; it has a high subsonic speed and a range of over 200 miles. The Quails are released by B-52s to simulate bomber images on enemy radars in order to aid bombers penetrating to their targets.

The last B-52s and B-58s were delivered to SAC in 1962, and for the first time since 1946 there were no strategic bomber aircraft being developed or produced in the United States. SAC bomber strength fell to 591 B-52s and 83 B-58s in late 1966, when the last B-47 bombers were retired (although 16 reconnaissance-version

RB-47s held on for a few months longer). Meanwhile, phaseout of the B-58s had begun, and all of those high-speed, short-range aircraft were gone by 1970. As the number of manned bombers declined, the expensive airborne alert program was also cancelled. The increasing number of dispersed Minuteman ICBMs in underground silos, and the completion of early warning systems that could provide at least 15 minutes warning of a Soviet missile attack, alleviated the need for the airborne alert. On the other hand, a large percentage of the planes were kept on 15-minute runway alert.

Also during the 1960s, these large strategic aircraft were employed in a conventional warfare role against Viet Cong positions in South Vietnamese jungles. On June 18, 1965, 27 B-52F bombers flying from Guam initiated strategic bomber participation in the Vietnam War. Subsequent B-52 raids conducted during the next seven years were considered highly effective in support of ground operations. The giant bombers were undetectable by Viet Cong troops in South Vietnam until their bombs were falling. Thus, the older B-52 aircraft were committed to the Vietnam War in a tactical role.

During the war period (1964-72), the overall B-52 force was reduced from some 625 aircraft to 450, although there were some qualitative improvements to the bombers through modernization. In the midst of this bomber drawdown, Secretary McNamara suddenly introduced a new "strategic" manned bomber, the FB-111. Immediately after the last B-52 and B-58 bombers were delivered to SAC in 1962, Secretary McNamara had requested the Air Force to "consider an alternative bombing system" as a follow-on to the B-52, B-58, and B-70 manned bombers. This would be an aircraft that would launch long-range, stand-off strategic missiles and would not have to penetrate the increasing Soviet bomber defenses. By the early 1960s, Soviet air defenses included over 4,000 jet interceptor aircraft and almost 8,000 surface-to-air missiles, with a continuing modernization program.

Then, two days after his announcement of further reductions of the SAC bomber force, on December 8, 1965, Secretary McNamara announced that the controversial swing-wing TFX "fighter" would be procured by SAC as a follow-on manned bomber. He directed that

210 aircraft be built in the FB-111 bomber variant.[25] The FB-111, like the B-58 Hustler and B-52 Stratofortress which it was replacing, would have to penetrate Soviet air defenses. In the event, only 76 of the FB-111 strategic bombers were built to equip four SAC squadrons, which fly 66 of the FB-111A aircraft.

The Strategic TRIAD

The third major US strategic system developed during the 1960s was the Polaris SLBM fleet. Together with land-based ICBMs and manned bombers, the Polaris submarines were considered the "third leg" of what has become known as TRIAD.

Although the Navy was initially opposed to large-scale Polaris development, a forceful Chief of Naval Operations, Admiral A. A. Burke, and his full endorsement of the project manager, Rear Admiral W. F. Raborn, got Polaris to sea far in advance of early schedules. By the early 1960s, the Navy was proposing a 45-submarine force (five squadrons of nine submarines each). Secretary McNamara, however, cut the planned force to 41 submarines (656 missiles), and the last Polaris submarine went to sea in April 1967, seven and a half years after the first. (Some 12 nuclear-propelled Polaris submarines were commissioned in the peak year of 1964, about the same number of Yankees completed in the peak year of the Soviet Yankee-class SLBM program.)

In the early 1960s, as the Polaris submarines joined the fleet, the Navy's 14 or 15 attack aircraft carriers were relieved of their primary nuclear strike role. The aircraft carriers do retain a nuclear strike capability, however, and continue to be a part of the nuclear attack plans.

The components of the US strategic offensive force developed during the 1960s, with differing origins, effectiveness, and operational

---

[25] Early estimates of the F-111 program provided for some 1,700 aircraft to be used by the US Air Force, Navy, and Marine Corps, and Australia and Great Britain. Because of subsequent dissatisfaction with the aircraft in some quarters, as well as budgetary constraints, only 442 were acquired by the US Air Force in the F-111 fighter variants through 1974, plus 76 FB-111 strategic bombers, and 24 aircraft for Australia. Adding in the few planes produced for the cancelled US Navy and British programs, the total F-111/FB-111 program through 1974 was approximately 550 aircraft.

Since the early 1950s, US aircraft carriers have made a significant—albeit often improperly understood—contribution to US strategic capabilities. During the 1960s, "flattops" such as the *Forrestal* class carrier *Saratoga* shown here had three squadrons of nuclear-capable attack planes among the 85 aircraft embarked. In addition, some fighter aircraft were fitted to carry nuclear weapons in the tactical or strategic role. *(US Navy)*

concepts, became linked together by the term TRIAD—after the fact
of their existence. The decisions of the 1960s with respect to numbers
of platforms would dictate the size of US strategic offensive forces in
the 1970s: 1,054 ICBMs, approximately 450 manned bombers, and
41 submarines with 656 missiles. In addition, forward-based tactical
aircraft in Europe and forward-deployed aircraft carriers could reach
the USSR with "tactical" nuclear weapons. While the size of the US
strategic offensive force in the 1970s was shaped by the deployments
of the previous decade, Soviet strategic weapon deployments were
continuing into the 1970s, and both superpowers soon would introduce new strategic weapons technologies.

6

Offense *Versus* Defense

During the 1960s, two aspects of strategic weapons began to dominate the arms race: ballistic missile defense and multiple warheads. The two issues are closely related in that each of these is a counter to the other. Before examining the chronology of events surrounding these concepts, it may be useful to examine the concepts themselves as dominant factors in strategic weapons development.

With the proliferation of ICBMs by the United States and Soviet Union in the 1960s, the amount of destruction that each side could inflict became enormous. Both superpowers had large proportions of their population and industrial capacity concentrated in cities. According to statements by Secretary of Defense McNamara, the destruction of 200 American cities could kill over half of the nation's population and eliminate three quarters of its industrial capacity, while the loss of 400 Soviet cities would mean that almost half of that nation's population and three quarters of its industry could be destroyed. The numbers of cities were counted in the hundreds, while the available nuclear warheads numbered in the thousands.

At the same time, technologies were becoming available that gave promise of an active ballistic missile defense whereby incoming ICBM warheads could be intercepted with Anti-Ballistic Missile (ABM) missiles. An active missile defense system consists principally of radars to detect and track incoming Reentry Vehicles (RV), and interceptor

59

DISTRIBUTION OF POPULATION AND
INDUSTRIAL CAPACITY (1970)

Number of cities	United States		Soviet Union	
	Percent of population	Percent of industrial capacity	Percent of population	Percent of industrial capacity
10	25	33	8	25
50	42	55	20	40
100	48	65	25	50
200	55	75	34	62
400	60	82	40	72
1,000	63	86	47	82

missiles to destroy these RVs. Formal US efforts to develop an ABM system began with the Army's Nike-Zeus system, initiated in 1956. Such a system could have become operational by 1963-64, but would —according to subsequent estimates—have been obsolete by that time. Other ABM concepts were put forward, including one that would permit Polaris-armed missile submarines to fire their weapons in either an offensive or ABM defensive mode. But research and development were undertaken only on the Nike-Zeus and its direct successors, the Nike-X, Sentinel, and Safeguard systems.

Soviet ABM efforts probably were formalized into a program shortly after the Nike-Zeus. Deployment of advanced defense systems, first reported near Leningrad in 1962, caused speculation as to Soviet ABM deployments, but these systems were later evaluated as advanced anti-aircraft installations. In 1964, the Soviets put on display an ABM missile labeled as the Galosh by NATO. Galosh missile launchers and associated radars subsequently were deployed around Moscow. Within three to four years, the system consisted of the large ABM-associated radars and 64 interceptor missiles, with one- or two-megaton warheads and an estimated range of 200 miles.

With this evidence of a potential Soviet ABM deployment, the United States initiated a counterdeployment of weapons to overcome ballistic missile defenses. The basic means to counter an ABM system are to saturate the ABM's radars and associated electronic equipment used to track incoming reentry vehicles, or else to exhaust the ABM interceptor missiles. Other methods, such as a preliminary attack on ABM radars (possibly by bombers), are less certain.

To overcome an ABM system, the number of RVs could be increased initially by increasing the number of offensive land-based or sea-based missiles. More missiles, however, meant more launch equipment, more crews, more submarines (for the SLBMs), more real estate (for the ICBMs), and so on. Instead, another technological approach to saturating ABM interceptors was undertaken, namely, the multiple warhead missile. With multiple warheads, a single missile carries aloft several RVs which are released in flight to come down separately against one or more targets. A simplistic analogy is the single, large bullet compared to a buckshot cartridge. The development of more accurate controls for rocket motors, computers, miniaturized electronics, and inertial navigation made multiple warheads feasible.

Multiple Warhead Development

The United States began deployment of the first multiple warhead on the Polaris submarine-launched missile. In 1964, the Polaris A-3 became operational. With a range of 2,500 nautical miles, the A-3 missile greatly increased the ocean areas in which Polaris submarines could operate and remain within missile range of Moscow and other inland Soviet targets. The A-3 variant carries a Multiple Reentry Vehicle (MRV) payload. As each Polaris missile streaks aloft, the warhead separates into three separate RVs, or "bomblets," that can strike a single target. Whereas the basic Polaris A-1 and A-2 warheads are generally described as being in the one megaton range, in the A-3's MRV configuration the three RVs have an explosive force of only 200-KT each, because of the additional weight and space required for the separation apparatus (the PBV or Post-Boost Vehicle). But although the sum of the three RVs is less than the Polaris A-1 and A-2 payload, the three RVs would impact on the target city or installation in a pattern that could result in greater overall destruction. The first Polaris submarine armed with multiple-warhead A-3 missiles, the

USS *Daniel Webster,* went to sea in 1964. Subsequently, most of the Navy's 41 ballistic missile submarines were rearmed with the A-3 missile.

But this missile, with its three MRVs, proved to be only an interim weapon. Development was already under way on Multiple Independently-targeted Reentry Vehicle (MIRV) warheads. Whereas the MRV warheads are "shotgunned" down onto a single target, with MIRV warheads each of the reentry vehicles or "bomblets" can be directed to a separate target. This separation is accomplished as follows. The rocket boosters carry aloft a "bus" containing the individual RVs. After the boosters burn out and fall away from the bus, the latter continues toward enemy territory, releasing the RVs in sequence. After each release, the orientation and velocity of the bus is changed by a preset program to aim the next RV release. Obviously, the area of land or "footprint" in which the separate RVs can be aimed is limited, and must fall within the overall range of the missile.

The first US tests of an operational MIRV system began in 1968 with the Minuteman-III, an ICBM with a nominal range of 8,000 nautical miles. Whereas the earlier Minuteman-I and II missiles carried a single warhead of about one megaton, the warhead of the Minuteman-III has three RVs with a yield estimated at from 170-KT to 200-KT each. Between 1970 and mid-1975, 550 of the earlier Minuteman ICBMs in the SAC arsenal were replaced by Minuteman-III missiles with MIRV warheads.

In 1970, the first submarine firings were conducted with the submarine-launched Poseidon C-3 missile. This MIRV weapon, the successor to the Polaris A-3 missile, has a reported range of 2,500 nautical miles and can deliver up to 14 RVs, each with a yield of about 50-KT. Between 1970 and mid-1978, the Navy planned to convert 31 of its Polaris submarines so as to enable each to fire 16 of the Poseidon MIRV missiles, generally carrying ten RVs. The ten oldest Polaris submarines are not suitable for modification to the newer weapon and carry the A-3 missile.

The Minuteman and Poseidon MIRV programs thus increased by more than fourfold the number of reentry vehicles of the US strategic offensive forces, easily providing the capability of overcoming any foreseeable Soviet ABM system and still destroy at least 400 cities. When the current US multiple-warhead programs are completed in 1978, the number of US long-range missile reentry vehicles will be as follows:

US STRATEGIC MISSILE WARHEAD CAPABILITY

Pre-MIRV	Post-MIRV
1,000 Minuteman	54 Titan
54 Titan	450 Minuteman-II
	1,650 Minuteman-III
656 Polaris	160 Polaris A-3
	4,960 Poseidon C-4
1,710	7,274

With respect to defensive systems, the US-Soviet agreement resulting from the Strategic Arms Limitation Talks (SALT) in 1972 restricted ABM deployments. Under this agreement, each nation was allowed to build and operate one ABM site in defense of the national capital and another in defense of an ICBM base. Each site was defined according to area, number of missile launchers, and types of radars. This aspect of SALT permitted the Soviet Union to maintain the Galosh ABM already emplaced around Moscow (which also defends some ICBMs in that area), and the United States to continue construction of a Safeguard ABM being installed near Grand Forks, North Dakota, to defend 150 Minuteman ICBMs. In SALT, the United States gave up a much-emaciated ABM program that was just put forward in 1967 to provide a full-fledged missile defense against Chinese Communist missiles, and then—in 1969—to defend the Minuteman ICBMs against a Soviet attack. On June 28, 1974, the allowable ABM sites were further reduced. Meeting in Moscow, President Nixon and Party Secretary Brezhnev agreed to retain only the ABM sites at Grand Forks and Moscow, and to give up the option of building a second site.

Another ABM concept that received consideration in the 1960s was the US Navy's proposal for a Sea-based Ballistic Missile Intercept

System (SABMIS). This concept provided for deploying SABMIS ships in the North Atlantic and North Pacific where their interceptor missiles could shoot down Soviet- or Chinese-launched ICBMs. The advantages of the forward-deployed ships would include early intercept, before multiple warheads fully separated and hence were easier to kill; moreover, the intercepts would take place over the sea and not the United States and Canada, and the launch of interceptor missiles would not interfere with ICBM launches from the United States, as would co-located ABM/ICBM systems. Studies indicated that the SABMIS ships—working either independently or with terminal defenses in the United States—would be both survivable and effective. But SABMIS was rejected, primarily because of US interservice policies which favored maintaining an Army role in continental air-missile defense; hence, only the (limited) Safeguard ABM program was put forward for consideration by the US government.

Multiple Warheads and First Strike

Virtually any technological development in strategic weapons accomplished by one side can be matched by the other, and so it has been with multiple warhead technology. On the Soviet side, the giant SS-9 Scarp provided a weapon to carry aloft multiple payloads. Testing of the SS-9 with a MRV warhead began in August 1968, and Western estimates soon credited the missile with the ability to carry three reentry vehicles of five megatons each. Thus, each RV was larger than any US ICBM warheads except the Titan-II.

Soviet multiple warhead development, even of MRVs that would be limited in coverage or "footprint" and targeting as compared to MIRV warheads, meant that the proposed US missile-defense systems could be overcome by saturation. Even discounting other Soviet ICBMs and possibly SLBMs, the Soviets could add RVs to the SS-9 force at much lower costs than the United States could add interceptor missiles to an ABM. With its huge payload, the SS-9 might ultimately be developed to carry as many as 25 RVs per missile (see Chapter 8).

Traditionally, intercontinental missiles have been viewed primarily for attacking opposing strategic offensive forces in a tactic known as

"counterforce." But the effectiveness of ICBMs carrying a single warhead could be limited against an enemy strategic force of about the
same size. ICBMs are susceptible to failures. For an ICBM to function
perfectly, hundreds of different parts must work within limited toler-
ances; although the percentage possibilities of individual failures are
small, in the aggregate they significantly reduce the effectiveness of an
ICBM force. In the late 1960s, Secretary of Defense Melvin Laird
judged Soviet ICBMs to have an effectiveness factor of 80 percent.
This meant that—on the average—one missile would launch, travel
to its target, come within expected accuracy, and detonate properly
eight times in ten firings. Hence, if a thousand Soviet ICBMs were
fired against one thousand ICBMs in the United States in a preemptive
strike, 800 of the Soviet weapons could be expected to destroy their
targets. This would leave the United States with about 200 ICBMs
ready to launch (assuming no US missiles were launched until after
the Soviet attack). Accepting the same 80 percent effectiveness for US
missiles, after absorbing a preemptive attack the US force could still
destroy 160 cities in the Soviet Union ($200 \times 0.8 = 160$). This
second-strike capability would destroy almost a third of the population
and over half the industry of the USSR.

The same arguments given above, but with the roles of aggressor
and victim reversed, would also serve to deter the United States from
launching a preemptive missile attack against the Soviet ICBM force.
Thus, one nation could always deter an enemy first-strike against its
ICBM force by maintaining the same number of ICBMs as, or a larger
number than, the opponent.

Multiple warhead deployments changed the counterforce equations.
With MIRV technology, the Soviets could conceivably arm 500 large
ICBMs with three warheads each, and with each having a yield of five
megatons and a quarter-mile accuracy.[26] Soviet leaders could then
plan a preemptive strike launching the 500 multiple-warhead ICBMs
against the thousand US missile silos. With an 80 percent reliability, some 1,200 RVs could be expected to strike their targets

---

[26] Measured in terms of Circular Error Probable (CEP), which is the radius of a circle within
which half of the RVs are expected to fall. According to official statements, the probability
of a Minuteman silo being destroyed by a five-megaton warhead is 50 percent with an accuracy of 0.6 miles, 80 percent with an accuracy of 0.4 miles, and 95 percent with an accuracy
of 0.25 miles. (Based on 1970 statements.)

(500 × 3 × 0.8 = 1,200), enough to "pose a serious threat to the survivability" of Minuteman, in the words of Secretary Laird. A surprise first strike of this magnitude could destroy almost all of the US land-based ICBMs; possibly ten or a score of US missiles would survive. But the Soviet Union would still retain some 500 missiles with which to threaten US cities, in the event that the United Sates should retaliate against the counterforce strike which—because of the fact that the ICBMs are emplaced in the midwestern states—would have killed relatively few Americans.

US authorities have not argued *if* such a situation could occur with MIRV, but rather *when* it could occur. Thus, multiple warheads have been a severely destabilizing influence on strategic weapons development. A leading US strategist, Dr. D. A. Paolucci, wrote as early as 1966 that MIRV technology was "fundamentally destabilizing":

> If the Soviets develop this technology, US nonmobile, undefended, land-based ICBMs become obsolete. They are too simple to target by Soviet counterforce. In such an environment, the only utility in nonmobile, land-based systems is a spasmodic retaliatory strike.
>
> In a MIRV world, sea-based systems—or mobile land-based systems—appear to be the only alternative available to insure a stable assured destruction capability.

7

The Other Nuclear Powers

US and Soviet development of strategic nuclear weapons was followed—as could have been expected—by British, French, and mainland Chinese programs.

Great Britain

During World War II, the United States and Great Britain collaborated on development of the atomic bomb. Because Britain was subject to German air attack at the time the decisions were being made, the actual research and development were undertaken in the United States. After the war, the US Congress passed the McMahon Energy Act, which precluded any exchange of information on the design of nuclear weapons between the United States and any other country. This legislation not only showed the United States determination to retain a monopoly of nuclear weapons technology as long as possible, but also helped shape initial US attitudes toward nuclear forces developed by the West European Allies. At the time, no other Western nation had either fissionable material or the means of manufacturing nuclear weapons.

British scientists—some of whom had worked at US atomic facilities during the war—produced the first British nuclear device, which was exploded on October 3, 1952, in an island group 50 miles north-west of Australia. It was another two years before actual weapons were available.

The first British-flown aircraft capable of delivering a nuclear weapon were 70 American-built B-29s transferred to the RAF Bomber Command in 1950. Powered by four piston engines, these bombers could have reached the Soviet Union with a nuclear weapon, if one had been available. These aircraft, designated Washington Mk I in British service, were discarded in 1954. The British conducted tests of atomic and hydrogen bombs in 1956-57 using the newly-delivered Valiant B Mk I aircraft. This was a four-jet, swept-wing bomber with a high subsonic speed and a strike radius of just over 2,000 miles. The first Valiant bombers entered service in 1955, and they served for nine years before metal fatigue failures caused their grounding in 1964 and subsequent disposal.

The Valiant, which was the first of the British V-bombers, was followed by the delta-wing Vulcan, which began entering RAF bomber squadrons in May 1957. This was also a four-jet aircraft, silghtly larger than the Valiant (200,000 pounds as against 175,000), but with a transonic speed (630 m.p.h. or Mach 0.95 at 55,000 ft.) and a strike radius of 2,300 miles (on high altitude missions). The initial Vulcan B Mk 1, which could deliver a free-fall nuclear weapon, was followed into service in 1962 by the slightly larger and higher-thrust B Mk 2 variant. This aircraft was fitted to carry the Blue Steel air-to-surface missile, credited with a range of 200 nautical miles while carrying a nuclear warhead. The third and last British V-bomber was the Victor, a four-engine crescent-wing bomber that entered service in small numbers beginning in 1958. With a performance similar to the Vulcan, the Victor also could carry the Blue Steel missile.

By the early 1960s, the RAF Bomber Command reached a peak strength of some 180 Vulcan and Victor aircraft, with many of the aircraft armed with the Blue Steel missile. However, even the 200-nautical mile stand-off range of Blue Steel was considered insufficient to overcome the increasing capabilities of Soviet air defenses. To extend the stand-off range and hence the survivability of the V-bombers, the British government negotiated to obtain the 1,000-nautical mile, air-launched Skybolt missile under development in the United States.

The Hawker Siddeley Vulcan flew in the strategic bomber role for the Royal Air Force during the latter 1950s and 1960s. With a high subsonic speed and medium combat radius (up to 2,875 miles), the aircraft could carry the Blue Steel 200-mile stand-off missile, free-fall nuclear bombs, or conventional bombs. Vulcans remain in RAF service in the strategic reconnaissance and tactical support roles. (*Royal Air Force*)

Shortly after the Skybolt test program began in 1962, however, the project was cancelled by Secretary McNamara for technical and economic reasons. This meant the end of the strategic bomber in the RAF.

In late December 1962, President Kennedy offered the British government the technology necessary to develop Polaris-armed, nuclear-propelled submarines. Previous US assistance had resulted in construction of the first British nuclear submarine, HMS *Dreadnought,* launched late in 1960. Thus, the decision was made in 1962 that Great Britain would go to an all-missile, seaborne deterrent.

In addition to strategic aircraft, several British tactical aircraft were fitted to carry nuclear weapons, including the highly effective, carrier-based Buccaneer, which remains in Navy and RAF tactical service. Another RAF nuclear strike aircraft, the TSR-2, was a Mach 2 aircraft which was to have had a combat radius in excess of 1,000 miles; the TSR-2 was cancelled before entering service.

Before moving to a sea-based strategic force, the British government did investigate land-based strategic missiles. Early in 1954, Britain undertook development of an IRBM fired from an underground silo. Named Blue Streak, this would be a second-strike or deterrent weapon, intended to ride out a Soviet attack. But because Soviet strategic weapons were based only 1,200 miles from Britain, sufficient accuracy would be available to the Soviets at an early date to destroy the Blue Streak IRBMs even in their hardened, underground silos. Accordingly, in 1960 the Blue Streak program was cancelled for both military and economic reasons. Simultaneously, the United States began establishing Thor IRBMs in Britain under joint US-RAF control. Beginning in 1958, some 60 of these 1,500-nautical mile nuclear weapons were emplaced in Britain. But the Thor system was short-lived, and the IRBMs were phased out by late 1963.

Britain had to rely on the remaining V-bombers for a strategic offensive force until the Royal Navy's first Polaris submarine was completed late in 1968. The submarine, HMS *Renown,* carries 16 Polaris A-3 missiles provided by the United States, but fitted with British-made MRV warheads. Originally, five submarines were planned (80 missiles), which would permit at least two to be at sea contin-

The Royal Navy developed a carrier-based nuclear strike force employing the Blackburn Buccaneer, shown here flying over HMS *Eagle*. The Buccaneer is believed to be the world's first aircraft designed specifically for low-level, high-speed strike. Capable of Mach 0.9 speeds, the Buccaneer has considerable combat radius and an excellent night/all-weather capability. (*Royal Navy*)

uously (with 32 missiles). But the plan for a fifth Polaris submarine was rescinded in February 1965 after the new Labor government took office. The fourth British Polaris submarine was completed in late 1969, enabled the Royal Navy to maintain at least one, and periodically two, Polaris submarines at sea on deterrent patrol. The nuclear strike responsibilities were formally transferred from the V-bombers to the Polaris submarines on July 1, 1969.

France

The French government initiated studies of strategic weapons immediately after the war. With the help of V-2 technology and German scientists, the French developed a missile designated *Véronique,* generally similar to the V-2 but unsuccessful for a strategic role. The development of atomic weapons followed; and on February 13, 1960, an atomic device was exploded in the Sahara Desert south of Reggan.

Reportedly, the French government approached the United States for assistance in developing missiles to deliver a nuclear warhead. No assistance was forthcoming, and programs were initiated to develop a land-launched missile (SSBS) and submarine-launched missile (MSBS).[27] As an interim strategic weapon system until the missiles became available, the French relied on the Mirage IV-A jet bomber developed in the 1950s. The Mirage IV-A is a delta-wing aircraft powered by two turbojets than can push the aircraft to a maximum speed of 1,454 m.p.h. (Mach 2.2 at 40,000 ft.), making it slightly faster than the fastest US strategic bomber, the B-58 Hustler (Mach 2.1). The French aircraft was considerably smaller (73,800 pounds *versus* 165,000 pounds), however, with about the same 1,200-mile tactical radius, which meant that it, too, required in-flight refueling from tanker aircraft to reach Soviet targets as far as Moscow or beyond.

The original Mirage IV-A flew in June 1959, but extensive redesign delayed introduction of the strategic bomber into combat squadrons until 1964. Some 36 Mirage IV-A bombers remain in strategic squad-

---

[27] *Sol-Sol Balistique Stratégique* and *Mer-Sol Balistique Stratégique,* respectively.

rons, each aircraft capable of carrying a single, free-fall 50-KT bomb.[28] Although the United States did not provide assistance in the development of the aircraft or weapon, several KC-135 tanker aircraft were transferred to France for use in maintaining the Mirages on airborne alert during crisis periods. Deployment of the 27 silo-emplaced SSBS missiles on the Plateau d'Albion began in 1971, and about two thirds of them were operational by the end of 1974. These weapons have a range of 1,500 miles and a warhead yield estimated at 150-KT.

The French third-generation strategic force consists of five nuclear-propelled submarines, each armed with 16 MSBS missiles. The French submarine force is interesting because the MSBS submarines introduced nuclear propulsion to the French Navy, whereas the US, British, Soviet, and Chinese navies all built torpedo-attack submarines with nuclear propulsion prior to embarking on missile submarine programs. Ironically, the submarine *Gymnote* had been started in 1958 as the first French nuclear submarine, but the project was cancelled; subsequently, the submarine was completed in 1966 with diesel-electric propulsion as a test platform for the MSBS missile.

All five French MSBS submarines, led by *Le Redoutable* completed in 1970, are to be operational by 1978, with at least two submarines (32 missiles) continuously at sea. The initial missile fitted in the early submarines is the MSBS M-1, with a range of 1,350 nautical miles and a warhead of about 500-KT. Planned improvements include an M-2 missile for the third, fourth, and fifth submarines. The M-2 version of the MSBS has a range of 1,600 nautical miles and improved penetration aids. Still more advanced MSBS concepts are under development to allow greater ranges, thermonuclear (fusion) warheads, and multiple warheads. As the MSBS submarine force becomes operational, the Mirage IV-A bomber force—like the British V-bombers—were to be shifted entirely to the tactical role.

This is an extensive strategic weapons program. Beginning after the British program, it has developed at an accelerated rate. In some respects, the French capability is superior to the British force (which now is limited to four SLBM submarines). Because of the lack of US

---

[28] The total Mirage IV-A program was 1 prototype, 3 preproduction, and 62 production aircraft.

assistance, the French program has cost considerably more resources than the British expended on their nuclear weapons.

China

Mainland China became the fifth nuclear power when it detonated a nuclear device in the desert area of Sinkiang Province in October 1964. Soviet military assistance to Communist China had begun with the Communist takeover in 1949, and soon extended to a number of armament and technological categories. In 1957, the Soviet Union agreed to provide China with extensive defense technology, technical assistance, and specialized training, including cooperation in atomic matters.

According to Khrushchev, the Soviets "packed up" a prototype atomic bomb and only at the last minute decided against sending the weapon to China. Khrushchev stated that:[29]

> We kept no secrets from them [the Chinese]. Our nuclear experts cooperated with their engineers and designers who were busy building an atomic bomb. We trained their scientists in our own laboratories.

By 1964, a small but efficient gaseous nuclear diffusion plant was completed at Lanchow;[30] and on October 16, 1964, the first Chinese nuclear device was exploded. Coincidentally, this was the same day on which Khrushchev was ousted as head of the Soviet government and Communist Party. His downfall was caused, in part, by the Sino-Soviet split.

Along with technical assistance, the Soviets provided the Chinese with weapons that could become "strategic" nuclear delivery systems in the context of a Soviet-Chinese conflict. The initial bomber aircraft in the Chinese Air Force were Soviet-supplied Il-28 Beagle light bombers. These were the same aircraft that Khrushchev had sent to

---

[29] Khrushchev, *Khrushchev Remembers—The Last Testament*, p. 268.
[30] Gaseous diffusion is the process whereby natural uranium is gasified to extract the relatively light uranium-235 atoms, suitable for core material in fission warheads.

Cuba in 1962. They could carry a single nuclear weapon about 1,200 miles on a one-way flight. Thus, Chinese-based bombers could barely reach the Soviet industrial centers of the Ural mountains, but not the major cities in European Russia. Obviously, these aircraft posed no threat to the United States.

About 1964, the Chinese assembled a Golf-class, diesel-electric-propelled missile submarine. The submarine was one of a number of Soviet-design undersea craft constructed in Chinese shipyards, initially with Soviet technical assistance and components. The single Golf SLBM submarine is considered operational by US intelligence analysts, but has never been fitted with ballistic missiles.

By the late 1960s, the Chinese Air Force was credited with having a few Tu-4 Bull piston bombers (copies of the American B-29). About a dozen of these bombers, which could reach targets in European Russia—if unopposed—may have survived in Chinese service into the 1970s. About 1970, the Chinese aviation industry began producing an indigenous version of the subsonic (Mach .85), jet-propelled Tu-16 Badger bomber. These were more effective aircraft than their predecessors. Production of both the Il-28 Beagle and Tu-16 Badger bombers continued through the mid-1970s, with about 200 of the light bombers and 60 of the medium bombers remaining in service. The sale of intercontinental Boeing-707 jet transports to China in the early 1970s provides the People's Republic of China with the technology for producing longer-range jet bombers.

The Chinese government gave considerably more emphasis to the development of ballistic missiles. The nuclear tests conducted during the later 1960s included at least one nuclear weapon carried by a ballistic missile. Deployment of Medium-Range Ballistic Missiles (MRBM) with a range of 700 to 1,000 nautical miles capable of delivering a warhead of about 20-KT was expected by the end of 1968. The deployments did not occur, however, possibly because of technical problems or the tumult caused by the Great Proletarian Cultural Revolution.

About 1970, there were indications that Chinese interest was shifting to a longer-range IRBM; and within the next few years, several ballistic missiles were deployed. Unofficial estimates credit the Chinese with a force of 20 to 30 MRBMs and 15 to 20 IRBMs by the mid-1970s. There is also an ongoing ICBM test program that could lead to an operational missile, with a range of perhaps 3,000 nautical miles, by the end of the 1970s. This weapon would be capable of reaching all Soviet targets as well as Asian cities, but they would not be a threat to the United States. At current rates of weapon development, Chinese ICBMs will probably not have sufficient range to strike targets in the United States until the 1980s. There are reports of Chinese construction of torpedo-attack submarines with nuclear propulsion; but the development of a significant SLBM capability also will not be a threat to the United States at least until the early 1980s, if then.

Now and for the near future, Chinese nuclear weapons must be considered a decade and more behind US and Soviet nuclear weapons technology. Still, the Chinese nuclear weapons capability is a distinct and increasing strategic threat to the Soviet Union and to Asian nations.

India

Beyond the five major world powers, observers have long speculated as to which nation would be the next to detonate a nuclear device. Candidates for this dubious distinction included Brazil, India, Israel, Japan, the Netherlands, Sweden, and West Germany. These nations and several others have been engaged in "peaceful" nuclear research efforts. India's efforts were aided by Canadian technical assistance and uranium.

India exploded a low-yield nuclear device in the Rajasthan Desert area on May 17, 1974. The Indian government promptly labeled the 10- to 15-KT explosion as "peaceful," and disclaimed any military intent. Semantics aside (for no one has yet demonstrated a peaceful use for a nuclear explosion), the Indian nuclear device does not constitute a strategic nuclear capability. At least for the next few years, the actual weapons and effective delivery platforms will be lacking. At this writing, the only strike aircraft in the Indian Air Force are British Canberra light bombers and Soviet fighter-bombers.

The acquisition of advanced strike aircraft, or even the use of existing aircraft in "suicide" attacks against Pakistani and possibly Chinese targets, are possibilities. But probably more significant are the implications for other nations. It may become politically necessary for the allies of Pakistan, India's traditional enemy, to provide nuclear weapons to that nation to maintain the "strategic balance" in the area. Zulfikar Ali Bhutto, head of the Pakistani government, declared that "if India builds the bomb, we will eat leaves and grass, even go hungry, but we will have to get one of our own." When Pakistan's first nuclear power plant was completed in 1972, with Canadian assistance, Bhutto pledged that Pakistan would use nuclear energy only for peaceful purposes. But after the Indian atomic test, a Pakistani official declared that his government was "reexamining its nuclear priorities."

Also in the wake of India's atomic blast, the Shah of Iran reportedly told the French magazine *Les Informations* that Iran was planning to develop nuclear weapons. A few days later, however, the Iranian Embassy in Paris published a statement, coinciding with the Shah's arrival in the French capital, that denied the earlier statement.

At this writing, the Iranian government was embarked on the development of what promises to be the most powerful military force in the Indian Ocean region. A short time before the Indian nuclear detonation, the Iranian government ordered 80 of the new US Navy F-14A supersonic fighters, as well as other advanced weaponry, some of which was not yet operational even with the US armed forces. In June 1974, the US government announced that it would provide nuclear power reactors to Iran. At the time, a US Department of State spokesman said: "We have no doubt that Iran does not intend to develop nuclear weapons." Iran may also purchase French-built power reactors, and has expressed interest in advanced reactor development, including the socalled breeder reactors, which produce more nuclear material than they consume.

Finally, there are periodic reports of nuclear weapons in Egypt, generally assumed to be Soviet-provided and under Soviet control, and in Israel, of indigenous manufacture. The Israeli government has denied that it possesses nuclear weapons; but on December 1, 1974, President Ephraim Katzir stated that Israel "has the potential" to make an atomic weapon, "and if we need it, we will do it." He did not state how long it might take Israel to produce the weapon, or under what circumstances it would be developed. The French-built research reactor at Dimona, Israel, can produce plutonium for nuclear weapons, and some observers have speculated that enough material had been produced through 1975 for the manufacture of five to ten nuclear weapons.

The most positive report that the Israelis possess nuclear weapons came in August 1975, when the Boston *Globe* reported that Israel had an arsenal of ten nuclear weapons. The writer was William Beecher, former defense writer for the *New York Times*, who had recently returned from a three-week trip to Israel and Egypt. Mr. Beecher's report had special significance; he had served as Deputy Assistant Secretary of Defense (Public Affairs) at the Pentagon from 1973 to May 1975. Still, at the time this monograph went to press, there was no official Israeli confirmation of the report.

Thus, as one US newspaper stated, India "let the nuclear genie out of the bottle." In some respects, nuclear weapons are only "bigger bangs" than conventional weapons; World War II destruction of Hamburg, Dresden, and Tokyo with conventional weapons tends to support this thesis.[31] But nuclear weapons also provide the opportunity for a single attacking bomber or missile to "leak" through a nation's defenses and, with one weapon, destroy an entire city. On the other hand, at the superpower level strategic weapons and RVs are measured and have impact in four-digit numbers.

---

[31] Atomic bombs killed an estimated 71,000 persons at Hiroshima and 40,000 at Nagasaki. Conventional bombing attacks killed 83,000 in Tokyo (March 9-10, 1945). 50,000 in Hamburg (July 24-August 3, 1944), and 130,000 in Dresden (February 13-14, 1945). Only rough estimates are available for the two German cities.

8

Today and Tomorrow: The Soviet Union

In the mid-1970s, both the United States and Soviet Union possess massive strategic offensive forces. Each nation has the capability of sustaining a massive first-strike attack, and still inflict unacceptable destruction upon the aggressor. Because of various qualitative and quantitative developments, both nations continue to procure these weapons. Among these developments are anti-aircraft and ABM technology to defend targets, increased missile accuracy and multiple warheads (MRV and MIRV) that threaten an opponent's strategic forces, and unproved weapons accuracy and variable nuclear yields that open a number of warfare options.

With these developments, the relative advantages and limitations of specific weapons have become more obvious. The United States and Soviet Union have developed similar as well as dissimilar strategic weapons. Comparisons of the superpower arsenals are clouded by the tendency of one side to appraise foreign developments in what is called the "mirror image" of its own efforts. For example, many US observers believe the Soviet long-range bomber force of some 150 aircraft to have the same mission as the US bomber force, which is more than three times larger, with significantly different aircraft, and different operating procedures. Or, what is the role of Echo-II cruise missile submarines operating in the Caribbean? Still another consideration is the impact on Soviet SLBM strategic capabilities if the SS-N-13 anti-ship ballistic missile is extensively deployed in Yankee SLBM submarines.

79

In short, simplistic comparisons have limited meaning. Trends, programs, and potential courses appear to have more relevance in attempting to understand the evolution of strategic weapons.

Land-Based Bombers

Perhaps the most difficult aspect of Soviet strategic weapons development to measure has been the *Aviatsiya Dalnovo Deistviya,* or Long-Range Aviation (LRA). The medium- and long-range bombers that became operational in the 1950s remain in service, although later, more capable variants have replaced the initial aircraft. In 1975, the LRA was estimated to operate:

    110 Tu-20 Bear long-range bombers
     35 Mya-4 Bison long-range bombers
    500+ Tu-16 Badger medium bombers
    200+ Tu-22 Blinder medium bombers

In addition, the Soviet naval air arm—*Morskaya Aviatsiya*—operates some 275 Badgers and a few Blinders in the strike role. Apparently, a large number of the LRA bombers as well as all of the Navy's Badgers can carry air-to-surface missiles, with the AS-3 Kangaroo missile (range 350 nautical miles), AS-4 Kitchen (250 nautical miles), and unnamed AS-6 (over 300 nautical miles) rated as having a strategic as well as anti-ship capability.

Generally, the LRA medium bombers are considered by US officials as being "theater" weapons. But by staging through bases in the Soviet Arctic, and with in-flight refueling,[32] these aircraft as well as the Bear and Bison bombers could reach targets in the United States. The naval strike aircraft, generally considered to have anti-shipping missions, also could be employed in nuclear strikes against the United States.

The possibility of the converse also exists, namely, that all LRA bombers as well as naval aircraft are "theater" weapons, intended for

---

[32] LRA operates approximately 50 Mya-4 Bison aircraft and some Tu-16 Badgers as tankers, and the Soviet naval air arm has about 80 Tu-16 Badgers configured as tanker aircraft. According to the British International Institute for Strategic Studies, about 75 percent of the LRA force is based in the European USSR and most of the remainder in the Far East, with staging and dispersal bases available in the Arctic.

use against land and sea targets in Europe and the regional seas around the Soviet Union. This indication is borne out, in part, by public statements of Soviet officials and by specific exercises. Soviet military and political leaders generally cite the Strategic Rocket Forces and the Navy as being the main striking power of the Soviet Union in the strategic context, without reference to LRA. Khrushchev himself, in the second volume of his memoirs, has cited various problems in the Soviet long-range bomber force. Discussing the Mya-4 Bison, he wrote: "This plane failed to satisfy our requirements . . . Our fliers didn't have much confidence in it. In the end, we decided to scrap the whole project." He also criticized the Tu-20 Bear, noting that ". . . it couldn't be used as a strategic bomber."[33]

Subsequently, naval exercises, including the multi-ocean "Okean" maneuvers of 1970, have employed LRA aircraft in anti-shipping roles, working in close collaboration with naval air squadrons. Still, the capability remains for a large number of Soviet bomber aircraft to reach the United States. Those not capable of returning to the Soviet Union could fly on to Cuba or Central America, or come down at sea, with their crews possibly being rescued by submarines.

The Soviet bomber force will probably remain at approximately current strength for the next few years. The LRA Bear-Bison bomber force has numbered some 150 aircraft for more than a decade;[34] the Badger-Blinder force has declined at the rate of some 20 aircraft per year for the past decade, but still has a respectable strength of almost 800 bombers. Now operational is a new "medium" bomber, the twin-jet Backfire which, like the US FB-111, is a variable-geometry or "swing-wing" aircraft. It has a maximum speed estimated at Mach 2. The Backfire is rated at approximately 275,000 pounds gross, or more than twice the size of the FB-111, but smaller than the B-1, an advanced strategic bomber being developed by the US Air Force (see Chapter 9). With an unrefueled combat radius of just over 3,000 miles, the Backfire rates as a medium bomber; but with inflight refueling or on one-way missions, the Backfire could reach targets throughout the

---

[33] Khrushchev, *Khrushchev Remembers—The Last Testament*, pp. 39-40.
[34] Reportedly, Bear-type aircraft still were being produced in small numbers into the 1970s, providing a continuing modernization program.

United States. (See Appendix A for a discussion of Backfire strike capabilities.)

Backfire bombers will begin entering Soviet LRA and Navy squadrons in the mid-1970s. Throughout the development of the Backfire, there has been some uncertainty as to the plane's primary mission. Replacing Badgers and Blinders, the Backfire will insure survival of the Soviet medium bomber force, although the role of Soviet medium bombers in strategic warfare cannot be definitely assessed.

Land-Based Missiles

Soviet ICBM deployments surpassed the US level of 1,054 land-based intercontinental missiles in 1969. Some US officials had anticipated that the construction of Soviet ICBM silos would cease at the point where the USSR had numerical equality with the United States. The rate of Soviet ICBM deployments did slow during the next few years, but deployments did not cease.

Soviet ICBM strength in 1974 was estimated at 1,570 missiles. A breakdown of the specific weapons has been estimated as:

    190 SS-7   Saddler (old)
     19 SS-8   Sasin (old)
    288 SS-9   Scarp (large)
    970 SS-11 Mod 1 (light—single RV)
     40 SS-11 Mod 3 (light—three RVs)
     60 SS-13 Savage (light)

There is no finite definition of the ICBM terms "large" and "light" in the lexicon of strategic arms analysts. Rather, "large" indicates the largest of the ICBMs in a nation's arsenal in terms of megatonnage, and "light" the lightest weapons. For the Soviet Union the SS-9, is a large weapon with a 25-MT warhead, while the SS-11 and S-13 are credited with warheads in the one- to two-megaton range. The multiple warhead on the SS-11 Mod 3 contains three MRVs of about 500-KT each.

The comparable numbers for US weapons are about ten megatons for the large Titan, and one megaton or less (with MIRVing) for the Minuteman missiles. This asymmetry in payload provides the Soviet Union with possibly as high as six times the megatonnage in ICBMs as the United States, although with only half again as many ICBMs.

ICBMs deployed by the Soviet Strategic Rocket Forces increased by more than 200 missiles per year between 1967 and 1971 (while US intercontinental missile deployments had halted at 1,054 in 1967). The rate of Soviet ICBM deployment slowed in the early 1970s, which gave rise to some speculation that the Soviets were about to reach their force level goal. (The number 1,618 was, in fact, agreed to as the upper limit for Soviet ICBMs in the SALT I Agreements.) There also was speculation that the Soviets would replace their massive ICBM deployment program with a qualitative improvement effort to provide improved accuracy and multiple warheads.

The first Soviet ICBM to display a multiple warhead was the large SS-9 Scarp. By 1970, there was considerable evidence that the Soviets had successfully tested the Mod 4 version of the SS-9, with a warhead that could carry three five-megaton reentry vehicles in a carefully spaced pattern. Even though the nominal 25-MT payload of the SS-9 is reduced to a total of 15-MT in the multiple warhead version to provide for the separation apparatus, the SS-9 Mod 4 still carries more megatonnage than the largest US strategic weapon. The three-RV configuration of the SS-9 Mod 4 immediately gave rise to speculation that the weapon was intended specifically for first-strike attacks against the Minuteman ICBM silos, which are arranged in patterns at an average of five nautical miles separation. Later statements by US officials indicate that the MRV-version of the SS-9 probably lacks the accuracy for attacking Minuteman silos, and has not been deployed in sufficient numbers to be effective against Minuteman.

The decline in the rate of Soviet ICBM deployments was followed by indications that new weapons would soon be available. New silos were identified that were not compatable with current Soviet ICBMs. In 1972-73, an intensive program of tests began for four new Soviet intercontinental missiles, the "light" SS-X-16, the "medium" SS-X-17 and SS-X-19, and the "large" SS-X-18.[35] Monitoring of Soviet tests of these missiles indicates that all (except possibly the SS-X-16) have MIRV warheads, and all carry higher-yield warheads than their predecessors. The five to eight MIRVs carried by the SS-X-18 are estimated to be approximately one megaton each. Up to 1975, the SS-X-16 had been observed in tests with only a single warhead. There are some indications that it may be a ground-mobile ICBM.

A critical question with these weapons is, of course, their accuracy. The previous generation of Soviet ICBMs was credited with less accuracy than their US counterparts. The higher numbers and higher payload of Soviet ICBMs can be an offset to US superiority in numbers of RVs and accuracy. Secretary of Defense Schlesinger discussed this aspect of Soviet ICBM development in these terms in April 1974:

> The Soviets have not had much experience to date with MIRVed systems. Consequently, I believe that they will have difficulties in getting the bugs out of those systems, and that they as yet have not appreciated the difficulties that they are going to have. So I tend not to talk about the next four or five years.

> What I am suggesting is that sometime in the 1980s, they may well have achieved a degree of accuracy and reliability in these systems that could cause an overall imbalance between their forces and those of the United States.

At the same time, Dr. Schlesinger also noted that:

> Given the warhead yield and CEP currently estimated for the MIRVed version of the SS-X-18, and looking at the fixed land-based portion of our strategic TRIAD in isolation from other elements, a force of about 300 of these missiles . . . could pose a serious threat to our ICBMs in their silos, even after those silos are upgraded. Moreover, it is more than likely that the MIRVed follow-on to the SS-11, whether it be the SS-X-17 or SS-X-19, will also achieve a respectable hard target kill capability during the early part of the next decade.

---

[35] The letter 'X' is deleted from this US designation of the missiles as they are deployed.

Commenting on these Soviet ICBM developments, Dr. Malcolm R. Currie, the Director of Defense Research and Engineering, stated late in 1974 that the "concentration of R&D effort needed for development of four all-new missiles, launch techniques, and new warheads far exceeds anything seen previously in the history of missilry." The best estimates available predicted that all four new Soviet ICBMs could become operational as early as 1975. The size of the Soviet ICBM program, in terms of both deployed missiles and research and development efforts, and Soviet superiority in missile payload demonstrate that the Soviet Union is embarked on an intensive effort to improve the quality and quantity of its ICBM program.

Although it is beyond the scope of this monograph to discuss national intentions in relation to strategic weapons, they do become pertinent as indications of certain developments. As discussed earlier, MIRV technology is destabilizing in that it offers the possibility of one ICBM force destroying another of similar size in a preemptive strike. US leaders have steadfastly disavowed any intention of developing an ICBM or other strategic force for a first-strike attack against a foreign strategic weapons force. (This is not to say that current and future US systems would not have some counterforce capability.) On the Soviet side, however, there are a significant number of statements reflecting an intention to employ strategic weapons against an opponent's weapons at the outset of a conflict. The Soviet Minister of Defense, Marshal of the Soviet Union A. A. Grechko, has stated:

> The [Soviet] Armed Forces must be capable under any conditions to frustrate a surprise attack by the aggressor with the use of nuclear as well as conventional weapons, and with *rapid, devastating blows to destroy his main missile-nuclear weapons* and troop formations, thereby assuring favorable conditions for the further conduct and victorious outcome of the war. [Emphasis added.]

The Soviet leadership is well aware of the value of surprise attack, and this is a main element of Soviet military doctrine for all services. The Chief of the Soviet General Staff, General of the Army V. G. Kulikov, recently noted that "surprise attack has always been an important principle of military art, and has frequently given the attacker decisive advantages in achieving victory."

Submarine-Launched Missiles

The massive Soviet ICBM deployments that began about 1967 were followed by a similar trend in SLBM deployments. The Golf and Hotel SLBM programs of 1958-62 had provided the Soviet Navy with 96 missiles in 23 diesel and nine nuclear-propelled submarines. The relatively short range of these weapons (300 nautical miles, and later 650 nautical miles), the requirement for surface launch with the earlier missiles, the operational mode of these submarines, and the anti-submarine forces of the US Navy made these submarines only a limited strategic threat to the United States.

The first "modern" Soviet SLBM submarine of the Yankee class went to sea in 1968. When the Yankee program ended in 1974, there were 34 of these submarines carrying a total of 544 SS-N-6 missiles with a range of 1,300 nautical miles. Subsequently, tests have been conducted with a 1,600-nautical mile, MRV-configured SS-N-6, apparently a weapon similar to the Polaris A-3 that releases three reentry vehicles onto a single target. In addition, the SS-N-13 ballistic missile, an anti-ship weapon with some form of terminal guidance, and compatible with the Yankee missile tubes, has also been tested. Although Yankees generally are considered to be "strategic" submarines, the sizing of the SS-N-13 to the Yankee again raises the specter that most Western military analysts may be completely misinterpreting a major Soviet weapons development.

By mid-1975, in addition to the 34 Yankee-class submarines, the Soviet Navy was reported to have at sea almost 15 of the follow-on SLBM submarines of the Delta class. The Delta submarine, with about 10,000 tons displacement and an overall length of almost 450 feet, is the largest undersea craft ever constructed. In the original configuration, the Delta has 12 SS-N-8 missiles with a range of 4,200 nautical miles. This means that without leaving Soviet territorial waters, Delta-class missile submarines can target many of the major cities of the

The Soviet Union's first "modern" SLBM submarine was assigned the NATO code name Yankee. Resembling Western strategic missile submarines in size and configuration, the Yankee apparently also has a tactical, anti-ship capability with the SS-N-13 ballistic missile. Like its Western counterparts, the Yankee carries 16 ballistic missiles and is fitted with torpedo tubes. The Soviet submarine is significantly faster.

In 1973, as the Soviet production run of 34 Yankee-class SLBM submarines neared completion, the Soviet Navy sent to sea the first Delta-class, nuclear-propelled missile submarine. This is the largest undersea craft ever built, with a length of almost 450 ft. It carries the longest-range shipboard weapon, the SS-N-8 missile, which can travel about 4,300 nautical miles carrying a nuclear warhead.

United States. The later Delta-class submarines carry 16 of the long-range weapons.

Soviet SLBM strength in mid-1975 could thus be estimated at about 50 modern submarines carrying 736 missiles (compared to 41 US Polaris/Poseidon submarines with 656 missiles). In addition to these modern submarines, there are the Hotel and Golf submarines which, although generally considered to be intended for use in Eurasian regions, can be—and have in the past been—deployed into the Western Hemisphere. These older submarines carry a total of over 90 SLBMs.

Like the Soviet ICBM program, SLBM force levels must be considered in the context of ongoing construction efforts. According to US estimates, in addition to the 45 completed modern submarines, there were another ten Delta-class submarines (minimum 120 missiles) being constructed in mid-1975. These submarines were expected to be at sea by 1976, raising the overall Soviet SLBM force to at least 55 modern submarines, with at least 796 missiles.

Under the terms of the SALT I Agreements, the Soviet Union must halt SLBM production with 744 missiles unless it is willing to phase out older, land-based SS-7 and SS-8 missiles in favor of submarine missiles. This replacement option would permit the replacement of some 200 older ICBMs with 200 SLBMs, with a total force level of 62 operational submarines and 950 missiles by mid-1977. At the current rate of production of about six SLBM submarines per year, the Soviet Navy could easily accomplish this mid-1977 force level. Soviet shipyard capability is rated as being able to build 12 of these nuclear-propelled, ballistic missile submarines per year, in addition to eight other nuclear submarines. With around-the-clock effort, the total rate of construction could be increased to about 30 nuclear-propelled submarines per year of all types.

There has been no indication in public sources that a multiple warhead has been tested for the Delta's SS-N-8 missile, and the Yankee's multiple warhead has not been reported as having a capability for striking separated targets. But the future development of MIRV warheads for SLBMs cannot be precluded in view of the experience that the Soviets are acquiring in current ICBM research and development efforts.

Although modern Soviet SLBM submarines physically resemble US Polaris/Poseidon submarines, there are several differences in their method of operation and hence possibly their employment. For example, the Soviet Navy does not now "double-crew" SLBM submarines in the manner of the US Navy, which alternates submarine crews in order to keep over 50 percent of the Polaris/Poseidon submarine force continuously at sea. Also, the Yankee submarines could have a major anti-ship capability with the SS-N-13 missile. In any event, it is clear that the overall Soviet SLBM program has enjoyed a high priority in Soviet planning. The Soviet military leadership regularly describes the submarine force in the same context as the Strategic Rocket Forces, and as being an intergral part of the long-range striking power of the Soviet Union. In 1969 or 1970, S. M. Lobov, the Commander-in-Chief of the Soviet Northern Fleet, which operates most of the SLBM submarines, was promoted to the rank of Admiral of the Fleet. He was the first Soviet officer to reach this rank while serving in an operational command. In 1972 or 1973, Admiral Lobov was appointed to the Soviet General Staff, the highest ranking naval officer ever to be assigned to that key body, and with the same rank as the Chief of the General Staff, General of the Army Kulikov. According to Professor John Erickson, a leading Western analyst of Soviet military leadership, Lobov's promotion was "designed to give the naval high command parity in rank with its opposite numbers in the Soviet strategic forces."

Other Weapons

In addition to the use of Soviet manned bombers, ICBMs, and SLBMs as strategic weapons, some US observers predict that the Soviet Union would employ other weapons in a strategic attack. These include the Fractional Orbital Bombardment System (FOBS), which the Soviets have flight-tested (employing the SS-9 missile to carry a payload aloft into a partial orbit), and the Multiple Orbital Bombardment System (MOBS), which, in the view of some experts in the field, would be an easy extension of the FOBS concept. With MOBS, the nuclear weapons are placed in full orbit prior to being de-orbited in a nuclear strike. There is also the continuing question of the strategic role of cruise missile submarines armed with the long-range SS-N-3 Shaddock missile. These weapons present a different and, in some circumstances, more difficult threat to detect than Soviet SLBMs.

Still another factor that should be considered in the Soviet strategic arsenal are the estimated 100 SS-5 Skean IRBM (2,300-mile/one megaton and 500 SS-4 Sandal MRBM (1,200-mile/one megaton) weapons. Although these weapons could not reach the United States, and some are presumed to be aimed against mainland China, they do provide the Soviet Strategic Rocket Forces with a capability for striking forward-based US weapons and strategic tanker bases in Europe, as well as British and French strategic installations. (At the same time, some US strategic weapons are targeted against Warsaw Pact military facilities and, of course, mainland China, and thus are not targeted against the Soviet Union.)

The difficulty in estimating Soviet capabilities is caused in large part by the asymmetries between US and Soviet strategic weapon systems. In the mid-1970s, the United States had advantages with respect to strategic weapons in (1) MIRVs and reentry vehicle technology, (2) guidance technology, and (3) nuclear weapons technology, that is, smaller weapons with a better yield-to-weight ratio. At the same time, Soviet advantages were in (1) numbers of launchers, (2) missile payloads, and (3) ongoing missile development programs. The Soviet Union's new ICBM programs give promise of overtaking the United States in number of separate warheads by the early 1980s. Although the Vladivostok Agreement of late 1974 limits each nation to 1,320 weapons with MIRV warheads, the payload of Soviet ICBMs would permit them eventually to deploy several times the number of reentry vehicles available to the US missile forces (see Appendix A).

The Soviet Union, according to Secretary Schlesinger, may in the future exploit the asymmetries that are in its favor:

We cannot exclude the possibility that future Soviet leaders might be misled into believing that such apparently favorable asymmetries could, at the very least, be exploited for diplomatic advantage. Pressure, confrontation, and crisis could easily follow from a miscalculation of this nature.

In this context, it is apparent that the Soviet leadership—which was always been impressed by sheer numbers—also perceives value in increasing the capabilities of strategic weapons, as evidenced by weapon deployments, observed research and development, and pronouncements of capabilities and intentions.

9

Today and Tomorrow: The United States

Current US strategic offensive forces are based on the TRIAD concept of three separate and distinct types of weapons, each of which is credited with being able to inflict "unacceptable" second-strike damage on the Soviet Union or any other nation that initiates a nuclear attack against the United States. The following discussion of the TRIAD components—land-based bombers, land-based missiles, and sea-based missiles—is presented in the order of their development.

Land-Based Bombers

Into the mid-1970s, the Strategic Air Command's bomber force consists of:

    80 B-52D
   165 B-52G
    90 B-52H
    66 FB-111A

These strategic bombers are supported by more than 600 KC-135 jet tankers. The last of the B-52s were manufactured in 1962, and the earlier B-52D variants are being extensively modified to prolong their service life. This update of B-52D aircraft will provide a 400-plane bomber force to operate through the 1970s. Although the B-52D bombers can deliver nuclear weapons, they are being updated and retained primarily to improve their conventional bombing capability.

According to official statements, only the B-52/H force (and presumably the FB-111 bombers) would attack heavily defended targets in a nuclear war because of their improved Electronic Countermeasure (ECM) equipment and bomber-carried Short-Range Attack Missiles (SRAM). The SRAM is a replacement for the Hound Dog missile. It is rocket-propelled, carries a nuclear warhead, and has a range of about 100 miles when released from high altitudes or 35 miles when dropped at low altitudes. Carried over enemy territory in bomber aircraft, the SRAM is intended to knock out enemy anti-aircraft defenses and to attack targets with intensive terminal defense. The B-52G/H aircraft each can carry 12 SRAM vehicles on two underwing pylons, plus another eight SRAM vehicles in the rear bomb-bay (in addition to four Mk 28 thermonuclear weapons in the forward bomb-bay). Four SRAM vehicles can be carried externally and two internally by the FB-111.

In addition to the use of advanced ECM equipment and the SRAM vehicles, the B-52G/H and FB-111 aircraft apparently require external assistance to penetrate heavily defended target areas. During the intensive B-52 bombing effort against North Vietnam in December 1972, 15 of the bombers were lost to enemy Surface-to-Air Missiles (SAM).[36] Between 50 and 70 SAMs were fired for each B-52 downed, an air defense effectiveness of only 1.4 to two percent. The B-52s were extensively supported by tactical fighter/attack aircraft that dropped radar-jamming chaff, electronically jammed enemy radars, and fired anti-radar missiles.

SAC bombers striking targets in the Soviet Union would encounter a more sophisticated air defense environment than in North Vietnam. At this writing, the Soviet air defenses included about 12,000 surface-to-air missiles on launchers, over 2,600 fighter-interceptors, numerous anti-aircraft guns, and an extensive radar warning and control system.[37] Many components have been battle-tested in Vietnam and the Middle East. Against this air defense environment, the attacking US bombers would be without the support of friendly tactical aircraft,

---

[36] Eight B-52s were lost operationally in the Vietnam War from 1965 to 1972; 15 were combat losses over North Vietnam during December 18-28, 1972, and one was lost over North Vietnam on January 3, 1973.

[37] Comparable US air defense forces in 1975 were 400 fighter-interceptors, all manufactured in the 1950s; there are no strategic surface-to-air missiles remaining in the US inventory.

would be attacking primarily from predetermined polar routes (many crossing extensive Soviet Arctic regions before reaching target areas), and would require aerial refueling en route to the target area. Still another factor is the potential vulnerability of the bombers to pre-emptive attack while on the ground at their US bases. The Soviet missile submarine force is the prime threat in this gambit, with the possibility that submarine-launched missiles could strike the bomber bases before the bombers, a portion of which are on runway alert, could take off.

Strategic bombers survive as a part of the TRIAD. There are sufficient differences between the situation of a strategic attack and a "limited war" for Secretary of Defense Schlesinger to state:

> We must be careful not to draw a false analogy from the Hanoi and Suez Canal air defense experiences. In both those cases, the air defenses were heavily concentrated in a very limited area; moreover, only conventional weapons were employed by the attacking aircraft. In the case of the Soviet Union, the number of places which have to be defended is very large and, consequently, the air defenses are spread over a vast area. Our bombers, in striking back at the Soviet Union, would be penetrating at very low altitudes to avoid the high and medium altitude SAMs, and would be using SRAMs to attack the low altitude SAM batteries. Moreover, our bombers would be employing nuclear weapons, only one of which need penetrate to destroy the target and probably much of its air defenses.

The existing B-52 force is predicted to "wear out" in the 1980s, when the newest of the aircraft will then be over 18 years old. The FB-111 is considered an "interim" strategic bomber, essentially forced on SAC by Secretary McNamara's need to increase the TFX/F-111 production base. To fulfill the perceived need for a manned bomber in the 1980s, the US Air Force is developing the B-1.[38] The B-1 is a low-altitude penetration bomber, designed to streak over heavily defended targets at high subsonic speed, launching stand-off missiles

---

[38] In 1962, the US military aircraft designation system was revised and the next bomber subsequent to the B-70 restarted the "bomber" series with B-1. During the concept stage the B-1 was known as the Advanced Manned Strategic Aircraft (AMSA).

(SRAM) and gravity thermonuclear bombs. Powered by four jet engines, the B-1 will be a large aircraft with a gross weight of some 390,000 pounds (compared to 480,000 pounds for the B-52G/H and 100,000 pounds for the FB-111A). Although at high altitudes the B-1 will have a Mach 2 speed, for low-level strategic attacks it would slow to about 600 m.p.h. The unrefueled combat radius is reported as 3,000 miles, meaning that the B-1 will need in-flight refueling from tanker aircraft to reach primary targets in the Soviet Union from bases in the United States.

The supersonic speed and advanced electronic equipment of the B-1 have led to an expensive aircraft, and cost is one of the major criticisms of the program. The first flight of the B-1A prototype aircraft took place in December 1974. The decision as to whether to start production was to be made during 1976. US Air Force proposals call for production of 240 B-1 aircraft. Many of their capabilities, such as the ability to seek out and destroy targets that survive an ICBM exchange, appear to have been overtaken by recent technological developments, including satellite reconnaissance, improved missile accuracy, and multiple warheads.

Soviet missile submarine development in the past decade has created the possibility of an SLBM attack on bombers on runways that has already forced dispersion of bombers and deployment of a coastal missile warning system. Age and speed limitations of current KC-135 tankers probably would force development and production of advanced tanker aircraft to support the B-1 bombers during the 1980s. Finally, Soviet air defenses are expected to continue to improve as new SAM systems, fighter-interceptor aircraft, and early warning and aircraft control equipment are introduced into the PVO. Proponents of manned bomber development point out that bomber survivability is valid on the basis of the difficulty that the Soviet forces would have in launching simultaneous preemptive attacks against all three components of the current TRIAD, especially the land-based ICBMs.

Although not generally considered in the context of strategic aircraft, the United States has tactical aircraft forward-based in Western Europe and South Korea, and forward-deployed aboard aircraft carriers that can reach some portions of the Soviet Union with small,

A prototype Rockwell International B-1A strategic bomber takes to the air. The four-jet, Mach 2+ aircraft was developed as a penetration bomber to strike deep into a heavily defended area with gravity bombs and stand-off missiles. Controversy over this role and increasing aircraft costs have added to the debate over whether or not to initiate production of 240 of these planes for the US Strategic Air Command. (*US Air Force*)

tactical nuclear weapons. The US Air Force currently flies the F-111 and F-4 Phantom fighters, which have a tactical nuclear capability. The former aircraft has the small, internal weapons bay common to the Air Force F-100 and F-105 "Century" series attack fighters. The F-4 Phantom, flown by a number of Western nations as well as Israel and Iran, can be fitted to carry tactical nuclear weapons on external pylons.

The Navy normally operates two large aircraft carriers in the Mediterranean and two or three in the western Pacific, each with some 70 to 100 aircraft. During crisis periods the number of carriers forward deployed can be increased to a majority of the 12 large carriers in service. All of these ships have squadrons of F-4 Phantom fighters and A-6 Intruder and A-7 Corsair attack planes that can be configured for delivering tactical nuclear weapons. It is not known at this writing how many aircraft or which type within the carrier air wings are rigged for nuclear weapons delivery. (The older concept of carrier-based "heavy attack" aircraft, developed through the AJ Savage, A3D Skywarrior, and A3J Vigilante, has been discarded in favor of smaller aircraft as the carrier's role in strategic warfare has been downgraded, the capabilities of smaller aircraft improved, and nuclear weapons technology developed.)

Land-Based Missiles

The Strategic Air Command operates 1,000 Minuteman ICBMs, 600 of which are being modified to the three-MIRV Minuteman-III configuration,[39] and 54 of the large Titan-II missiles. These weapons are in partially protected underground silos in the western portion of the United States. They are solid-propellant ICBMs that can be launched on short notice to strike targets in the Soviet Union or mainland China with a flight time of less than 30 minutes (compared to several-hour flights for manned bombers).

These 1,054 ICBMs have a potential of delivering a total of 2,154 RVs against the Soviet Union. Most of these are small weapons, about

---

[39] In September 1974, Secretary Schlesinger approved the deployment of 50 additional Minuteman-III missiles; previously, the Minuteman mix had been authorized at 550 Minuteman-III and 450 Minuteman-II missiles.

A variable-geometry (swing-wing) B-1A climbs aloft with an F-111, the tactical strike version of the FB-111A medium-range strategic bomber. Both aircraft sweep back their wings for high-speed flight, and extend them (as shown here) for takeoff, cruise flight, and landing. F-111s were used in the tactical strike role in Vietnam. (US Air Force)

200-KT for each of the Minuteman III reentry vehicles, and about one megaton for each Minuteman-II warhead. The 54 large Titan-II weapons each have a warhead of about 10-MT. Thus, the land-based ICBM force provides both a large number of RVs and, in the few Titan-II missiles, large warheads.

The principal threat to the Minuteman-Titan ICBMs is the potential of a preemptive attack by Soviet land-based ICBMs against the US weapons while the latter are still in their underground silos. Soviet SLBMs—for the near future, at least—lack the accuracy needed to zero in on the underground missile silos. According to US defense officials, the Soviet Strategic Rocket Forces could become a threat to US missile survivability by a continued proliferation of ICBMs, by increases in accuracy, or by MIRV developments. Lieutenant General W. P. Leber, US Army, manager of one phase of the US ABM program,[40] has stated that even the current Soviet ICBM inventory of about 1,600 missiles, "with improvement of accuracy alone . . . could reduce Minuteman survivors to unacceptable levels." Similarly, future increases in missile numbers or extensive MIRV efforts could present an overwhelming threat to US land-based missiles.

Possible defenses against this threat include further hardening of Minuteman-Titan silos, replacement of fixed ICBMs with mobile ICBM launchers on railway trains or motor trucks, deployment of additional silo-based ICBMs, or installation of defensive ABM missiles. At this time, proposals are being considered for both the hardening of silos and the installation of defensive missiles. The SALT I Agreements provide for a single Safeguard ABM site to defend 150 of the Minuteman missiles. Both of the defensive options, hardening and defensive missiles, can be overcome by available technology (increased RV accuracy and increased RV numbers, respectively). Neither of these potential Soviet "counterforce" options are restricted by SALT I and, because they are qualitative rather than quantitative in nature, are difficult to control.

A final factor in US Minuteman-Titan ICBM effectiveness is the question of reliability. Of the three components of the current TRIAD,

---

[40] In addition to the Safeguard ABM concept, the US Army currently has under development the Site Defense Program for possible deployment in defense of ICBM silos.

the land-based ICBMs are the only force that has not been extensively tested. Bombers regularly take off, fly missions, and drop bombs; prior to test-ban agreements, bombers even dropped nuclear weapons. Similarly, submarines regularly fire unarmed Polaris and Poseidon missiles on test ranges; and on May 6, 1962, the USS *Ethan Allen* fired a Polaris A-1 missile almost 1,200 nautical miles in the Pacific with a nuclear detonation. No ICBM has been fired from an operational silo. Periodically, the silo crews have fired various ICBMs from test facilities at the Vandenberg Air Force Base in California and from Cape Kennedy in Florida under highly controlled conditions. But periodic efforts to launch an ICBM with reduced fuel and no warhead from an operational silo have failed, and Congress has refused approval of full-range test firings from an operational silo that would take the missile over urban areas.

Beyond the replacement of earlier Minuteman missiles with the MIRV-carrying Minuteman-III, there is no specific follow-on ICBM deployment program in the United States. During 1966-67, the Department of Defense conducted a technical study of future ballistic missiles. Known as the STRAT-X study, it recommended—from numerous candidate weapons—the development of four advanced strategic systems, two land-based and two sea-based. The land-based weapons were ICBMs in hard-rock silos and ground-mobile ICBMs; the sea-based systems were a long-range missile in an advanced submarine (originally known as ULMS for Underwater Long-range Missile System), and a surface-ship missile system. Of the four, only the ULMS concept survived; in modified form, it is the current Trident program.

With neither of the land-based missile concepts of STRAT-X pursued, US research and development efforts related to the ICBM force have concentrated in specific technology areas, among them the ABRES (Advanced Ballistic Reentry System) program, refinements in the existing Minuteman guidance system that could increase accuracy, development of higher-yield RVs for the Minuteman-III (designated Mk 12A), and research into providing the Minuteman-III with a larger number of small RVs (the Pave Pepper program). The Navy is developing the Mk 500 Maneuvering Reentry Vehicle (MaRV) that could be compatible with both the Trident SLBM and

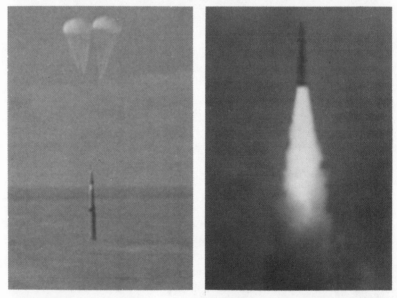

An advanced strategic weapons concept successfully tested by the US Air Force in the Fall of 1974 is shown here. A Minuteman ICBM is pulled in its cradle from a Lockheed C-5A Galaxy transport by parachute, stabilized in midair, and then fired for a few seconds. The tests demonstrated the feasibility of launching large ballistic missiles from transport-type aircraft. A future nonpenetration strategic bomber might attack an enemy nation from beyond its defenses with long-range ballistic and cruise missiles. *(US Air Force)*

Minuteman ICBM. A final consideration for improving the effectiveness and survivability of ICBMs is the airborne launch concept. During the Fall of 1974, concrete slabs simulating a variety of missile weights, and then an 86,000-pound Minuteman-I missile, were test-dropped by parachute from huge C-5A transport aircraft; and the Minuteman-I missile was ignited briefly to test its first-stage engine. The evaluation was technically successful. This concept, although more flexible and hence possibly more survivable than a fixed, land-based ICBM, is considerably more expensive to maintain. Moreover, the air-launched ICBM can be assumed to have less accuracy than a land-based or sea-mobile ICBM.[41]

These and other research and development efforts should, in the view of ICBM proponents, enable the Minuteman system to survive as an effective strategic weapon well into the 1980s.

Submarine-Launched Missiles

The third component of the current TRIAD to be developed was the Submarine-Launched Ballistic Missile (SLBM) force, which now consists of ten nuclear-propelled submarines armed with the Polaris A-3 missile (160 missiles), and 31 submarines armed with the Poseidon C-3 weapon (496 missiles). At any given time, just over half of these submarines are at sea with their missiles in a very high degree of readiness.[42]

Any major threat to the Polaris-Poseidon SLBM force that may emerge would probably come from Soviet Anti-Submarine Warfare (ASW) forces. Soviet fleet development has been multifaceted, and includes both offensive and defensive components. Certain components, such as the large, graceful, and heavily armed helicopter ships

---

[41] The concept of air-launching strategic missiles was previously examined by the US Air Force with the Rascal (13,000 lbs), Skybolt (11,300 lbs), Navaho (120,500 lbs), and current SRAM missiles. An aircraft proposed in the late 1950s to carry two Navaho missiles on airborne alert, called the XC-Heavy, was so large that its landing gear track would have permitted it to use less than a dozen airfields in the world. An alternative payload for the XC-Heavy would have been a single 160,000-pound B-58 bomber!

[42] In these calculations, the Polaris A-3 is considered as a single weapon, although actually three MRVs are aimed at the same target. US Navy SLBM submarines normally are at sea for 60 days and in port for 30 days; the number of submarines normally at sea is less than two thirds of the force, however, because of submarines in overhaul (including nuclear refueling), training, missile tests, and so forth.

Moskva and *Leningrad*; the nuclear-propelled torpedo-attack sub-marines; and the computer-equipped I1-38 May ASW aircraft, prob-ably were developed for anti-Polaris/Poseidon operations. But Soviet ASW capabilities are one of the more difficult aspects of Soviet power to understand. For example, the Soviet Navy has not pursued the development of large surface-ship sonars, as the US navy has done; while there is evidence that the Soviets are investigating such diverse aspects of ASW as satellite and psychic detection, and the pos-sibility has been suggested that the Yankee/SS-N-13 system has an anti-submarine role.

Most authorities appear to agree that Soviet ASW is not now, nor for the near future, capable of destroying a significant portion of the Polaris/Poseidon submarine force. Senior defense officials rarely speak in terms of absolute effectiveness or the absolute survivability of any one strategic weapon. Yet, in 1970, Secretary of Defense Laird did state that:

> According to our best current estimates, we believe that our Polaris and Poseidon submarines at sea can be considered vir-tually invulnerable today. With a highly concentrated effort, the Soviet Navy today might be able to localize and destroy at sea one or two Polaris submarines. But the massive and expensive undertaking that would be required to extend such a capability using any currently known ASW techniques would take time and would certainly be evident.

In considering potential anti-Polaris/Poseidon efforts, it should also be remembered that attacks against submarines would not attract nuclear warheads to US territory, as would preemptive strikes against land-based bombers or ICBMs.

Two factors probably will reduce Polaris/Poseidon effectiveness in the future: Soviet ASW efforts and the aging of US submarines. In this regard, Secretary Laird's 1970 statement also noted:

> However, a combination of technological development, and the decision by the Soviets to undertake a worldwide ASW effort, might result in some increased degree of Polaris/Poseidon vul-

nerability beyond the mid-1970s. I would hope that Polaris would remain invulnerable at least through the 1970s. But, as a defense planner, I would never guarantee the invulnerability of *any* strategic system beyond the reasonably foreseeable future, say five to seven years.

With respect to aging, the Navy's 41 missile submarines were completed from 1960 to 1967; by 1980, the oldest submarines will have had 20 years of high-tempo operations. In time, submarine machinery noise levels increase; and at the same time, ASW detection capabilities improve. Moreover, the ships simply wear out after 20 to 30 years of operation. These factors led to the STRAT-X study of 1966-67, which recommended two advanced sea-based strategic missile systems, one surface and one submarine; the latter was the Undersea Long-range Missile System (ULMS). Subsequently approved for development as the Trident SLBM, ULMS provides for an advanced submarine with improved quieting and other features not available in the older Polaris/Poseidon undersea craft, and an advanced, multi-warhead missile with a range of about 6,000 nautical miles. With that range, a Trident SLBM submarine could cruise in the western Atlantic or western Pacific oceans and still have Moscow within range of its weapons. These oceanwide operating areas would make most Soviet ASW efforts, of whatever nature, more difficult than ASW efforts against Polaris/Poseidon submarines, which have a maximum missile range of about 2,500 nautical miles.

The surface missile ship proposal was not approved for development. Periodically, the Navy has studied the feasibility of installing strategic missiles on surface ships, both warships and merchant-type ships. The Surface Launched Missile System (SLMS) of the STRAT-X study and Ballistic Missile Ship (BMS) concepts provide for either IRBMs, such as the Polaris or Poseidon, or longer-range Minuteman ICBMs to be installed in fast (20- to 30-knot) merchant ships. Having the appearance of commercial cargo ships, the missile-armed merchantmen could operate in world shipping lanes, and would require large increases in Soviet countermeasures. Reportedly, studies indicated that shifting of Minuteman ICBMs from underground silos to modular launchers in merchant-type ships would significantly increase their survivability from Soviet preemptive attacks, and would also

This is a rare surface firing of an SLBM from the USS *Henry Clay*, one of the US Navy's 41 Polaris-Poseidon missile submarines. The US Navy has begun the Trident SLBM program, providing initially for ten very large submarines (560 feet long compared to 425 feet for the *Henry Clay*), and a long-range missile (with a range of 4,000 nautical miles, as compared to 2,500 for the Polaris-Poseidon). When the first Trident submarine becomes operational in the early 1980s, the Soviet Navy will have at least 52 modern SLBM submarines, about one third of them armed with 4,300-nautical mile SS-N-8 missiles. *(US Navy)*

enable them to target the Soviet Union from any broad ocean areas. Nevertheless, the SLMS/BMS option was deferred.

On the other hand, the ULMS/Trident program was initiated. In early 1972, Secretary Laird told the Congress that: "I have carefully reviewed all alternatives for new strategic initiatives, and have decided that acceleration of the ULMS program is the most appropriate alternative, since the at-sea portion of our sea-based strategic forces has the best long-term prospect for high pre-launch survivability."

The Trident program has developed into two phases, the first to provide a MIRV missile with a range of about 4,000 miles for installation in the later Polaris/Poseidon submarines during the late 1970s, and then a new nuclear-propelled submarine, the first of which would become operational about 1980, with ten such submarines now planned. The original ULMS concept, as proposed under STRAT-X, has been degraded somewhat by the new submarine, which is of conservative design, and essentially an enlargement of the Polaris/ Poseidon type, with limited improvements in performance. Probably the Trident submarines will replace the ten oldest Polaris submarines, which are not suitable for Poseidon conversion, and thus would provide an SLBM force of 41 submarines and 736 missiles at sea by the mid-1980s.[43]

No development work has been undertaken on the longer-range (6,000 nautical mile) submarine missile, as research in this field has concentrated on the Trident-I missile, which is adaptable to the Poseidon submarines. This interim missile configuration will, in time, partially dictate the design of the Trident submarine and Trident-II missile.

The high cost and large size of the Trident submarine has led Secretary Schlesinger to initiate design efforts for a new and less costly SLBM submarine, tentatively known as the "Narwhal" program, because of its use of the same kind of nuclear reactor as in the submarine *Narwhal*. This submarine, which could carry 16 Trident-I

---

[43] The SALT I Interim Agreement, which was to expire in 1977, requires the US to phase out an equivalent number of strategic missile launchers (Polaris or Titan) as each Trident submarine enters sea trials.

missiles, was proposed as a low-cost replacement for aging Poseidon submarines during the 1980s. As envisioned, the *Narwhal* design would complement the Trident submarine, although criticism of the size and cost of the latter led to speculation that the smaller *Narwhal* type may become the successor to the Polaris/Poseidon submarines. Congressional opposition to developing a second Trident submarine class simultaneous with the first led to cancellation of the *Narwhal* design.

Current US Department of Defense planning apparently provides for the following strategic weapon deployments by the latter 1980s under current US-Soviet agreements, which limit each side to 2,400 delivery vehicles:

240	B-1 manned bombers
approximately 200	B-52 and FB-111 manned bombers
1000	Minuteman ICBMs
54	Titan ICBMs
240	Trident SLBMs (in 10 submarines)
496	Poseidon SLBMs (in 31 submarines)
160	Polaris SLBMs (in 10 submarines)

Obviously, the age and condition of the Titan missiles and Polaris submarines will probably preclude their consideration as first-line weapons in the latter 1980s; more likely, they will be discarded by the late 1970s and early 1980s, respectively.

Tomorrow's Options

The United States appears to be committed to the TRIAD of strategic weapon systems—manned bombers, ICBMs, and SLBMs. Each of these systems has sufficient reentry vehicles and megatonnage to devastate the Soviet Union. The rationale for maintaining these somewhat duplicative systems has been primarily to insure survival of a second-strike capability against a Soviet preemptive attack. The logic is as follows. Although the Soviets could launch attacks against one or possibly two of the TRIAD forces, simultaneous attacks against all three would be impossible. The TRIAD forces have differing vulnerabilities dependent, in part, upon one's point of view, on predicted

Soviet weapon capabilities, and on the characteristics of follow-on TRIAD systems, such as the B-1 bomber and Trident missile submarine.

It is beyond the scope of this outline to propose future TRIAD force mixes or force levels. But the question must be raised, Is TRIAD, a concept evolved after the fact more than a decade ago, providing the United States with adequate assured destruction forces in the coming decade? Some of the factors that bear on an answer to this question include the relative survivability and effectiveness of one or two strategic forces as against the existing TRIAD. Or, in view of probable Soviet developments, should the nature of the current TRIAD components be changed? For example, instead of a penetration aircraft, should the successor to the B-52 manned bomber be a stand-off aircraft, remaining outside the Soviet air defenses and releasing Air-Launched Ballistic Missiles (ALBM) or Air-Launched Cruise Missiles (ALCM)? Or, could Submarine-Launched Cruise Missiles (SLCM) provide a more viable deterrent force, in conjunction with the *Narwhal*-design ballistic missile submarine concept, than a force of only the larger Trident missile submarines?[44]

In general, mobile systems (now bombers and submarines) are more likely to survive first-strike attacks than fixed land weapons, and they can be more readily tested. Sea-mobile systems have the further advantage of removing strategic weapons from national territory (called "value"), so that an enemy attack—rational or irrational—against US strategic forces will not impact RVs on the United States. But mobility is expensive, and systems such as bombers and submarines are considerably more costly to operate than fixed-silo ICBMs.

Still another consideration in strategic weapons systems planning must be flexibility. With the Soviet development of nuclear and thermonuclear weapons, it became apparent that the United States required more flexible responses to possible hostile actions. President Nixon has stated:

---

[44] The ALBM, ALCM, and SLCM concepts currently are under study; all appear to be feasible for development and deployment in the near future. The US Air Force conducted flight tests of ICBM launchings from C-5A large transport aircraft late in 1974. The Soviet Union currently operates ALCM and SLCM weapons that probably have strategic roles (see Appendix C).

No President should be left with only one strategic course of action, particularly that of ordering the mass destruction of enemy civilians and facilities. Given the range of possible political-military situations which could conceivably confront us . . . we must be able to respond at levels appropriate to the situation.

Accordingly, US national leaders should have the means—both weapons and strategy—at least to consider a scale of options between all-out nuclear war and absolute capitulation. Some of these means probably involve more accurate weapons which often have been cited as representing a first-strike capability. Obviously, other choices, such as large numbers of missiles or reentry vehicles, could similarly be interpreted as providing a first-strike capability, should one wish to consider them in that context.

Modern weapons are complex, and so are the problems of strategic weapons planning for the future. Traditional confidence in "our way is the right way," whether on a national or service basis, is no longer an adequate approach. Certain factors are predictable. Weapons accuracy will improve, and weapon yields will become greater as well as smaller. But there is one factor which is absolutely immutable. The sea will continue to offer a potential operating area of 70 percent of the earth's surface, compared to about six percent available for basing options in the United States. Less predictable are sensor and guidance capabilities. Similarly, future Soviet technological developments and strategy cannot be predicted with certainty. For example, deployment of the large SS-9 missile did not reach the levels of Western intelligence predictions; while Yankee-class submarine construction rates exceeded estimates, and there is a serious question of the possible anti-ship role of some of these submarines (with the SS-N-13 missile). In addition, deployment of the SS-17, SS-18, and SS-19 ICBMs—all estimated to be operational in 1975—could provide the Soviets with the means of delivering several times the number of MIRV warheads to the US.

In this environment, continued intelligent and rational discussion and analysis of the issues involved are vital to the national security of the United States.

Appendix A

Statement of Chairman, Joint Chiefs of Staff[45]

Over the years, the Secretary of Defense and my predecessors have noted that the relative US strategic power had peaked and was on the decline; that we are approaching parity; and finally, that the balance was in dynamic equilibrium. The static measures of relative military strength today remain in rough equilibrium. But in a technological era marked by giant strides in both science and engineering, we must approach the future with firmness and caution—firmness in our resolve to stabilize the static balance, and caution in minimizing the chance of technological surprise.

There is mounting evidence that the Soviet Union is pressing forward vigorously with massive programs for near-term deployments involving every facet of offensive strategic power. At the same time, it is improving appreciably, at a more gradual rate, capabilities for strategic defense and pursuing with firm determination development of advanced technology appropriate to the entire strategic equation.

The Soviet Union's focus is not simply on maintaining the current advantage in terms of megatonnage and throwweight, but it applies as well to accuracy, flexibility, survivability, and MIRVing intercontinental missiles.

At the SS-9 complexes, work is under way which will permit the deployment of the heavier, more accurate, and more lethal SS-18.

---

[45] Extracted from General George S. Brown, USAF, "United States Military Posture for FY 1976" (1975), pp. 7-47.

111

SS-11 silos have been or are in the process of being prepared for the SS-17 and the SS-19. Both are MIRVed, more accurate, have increased throwweight, and are more survivable than the SS-11s they are designed to replace. The SS-X-16 is judged to have appreciably greater throwweight and accuracy than the SS-13 it apparently will replace. It has many indications of being deployable as a mobile system as well. The SS-7 and the SS-8 appear destined for replacement under the terms of the Interim Agreement by modern, probably improved, SLBMs, perhaps with multiple warheads displaying greater accuracy, although their throwweight and yield are somewhat reduced. These SLBMs will be deployed, not on the modern Delta submarine alone, but upon a modified "super" Delta carrying many more missiles than the 12-tube standard Delta.[46] Hardened ICBM launch control facilities have been constructed and the program continues. A new airborne command post is probably operational. The multipurpose Backfire bomber is entering the operational force. Research and development continues. On the defensive side, the Soviet Union continues to improve the capability of current forces. It is deploying improved equipment such as the MiG-25 interceptor, a product-improved SA-5 (surface-to-air missile), and new warning facilities. Research continues on new ABMs. Each of these systems and the US program will now be examined in some detail.

US-USSR ICBM Forces

Placing the ICBM balance in proper perspective requires a brief conceptual consideration of the legal constraints upon ICBMs flowing from the Interim Agreement on Strategic Offensive Arms which, under the Vladivostok framework, will remain in force until October 1977, when the new agreement incorporating relevant provisions will come into effect.

The Interim Agreement prevents the construction of new ICBM fixed, land-based launchers after 26 May 1972, and limited the conversion of the then existing silos to modernization and replacement

---

[46] The improved Delta-class submarine subsequently has been described as carrying 16 SS-N-8 missiles.

which would not increase the existing dimensions of land-based ICBM silo launchers more than 10 to 15 percent. The Agreement also prohibits converting any of the ICBM launchers deployed prior to 1964 (e.g., SS-7, SS-8, and Titan-II) or launchers for "light" ICBMs (e.g., SS-11 and Minuteman) into launchers for "heavy" ICBMs deployed after 1964 (e.g., SS-9). The Soviet negotiators refused to agree to a common definition of a "heavy" missile. The United States, however, inserted into the record its understanding that any ICBM having a volume significantly greater than the largest "light" ICBM then operational, i.e., the SS-11, would be considered a "heavy." Other than silo size and the mix of light and heavy missile launchers, there was no limitation on qualitative factors or research, development, or testing.

Chart 1 presents scale drawings and individual characteristics of the US and USSR ICBMs currently deployed or undergoing flight tests.

SS-7 and SS-8

The SS-7s and 8s are both pre-1964 "heavies." Launchers for the 190 SS-7s are deployed at hard and soft sites. The 19 SS-8s likewise are deployed at both hard and soft sites.

You will recall that the Protocol to the Interim Agreement permits the conversion to SLBMs of ICBMs deployed prior to 1964. It is our belief that all 209 SS-7 and SS-8 launchers will eventually be phased out for this purpose.

SS-9

The SS-9 is a very large liquid-fueled missile with a combination of accuracy and yield giving it a significant capability to destroy silos, command and control facilities, and other hard targets. There are four variants of this missile. All have single warheads except the MRV MOD 4, which has three. The MOD 3 remains an enigma. It has been tested in both a depressed trajectory and in a fractional

CHART NO. 1

COMPARISON OF US AND USSR ICBMs

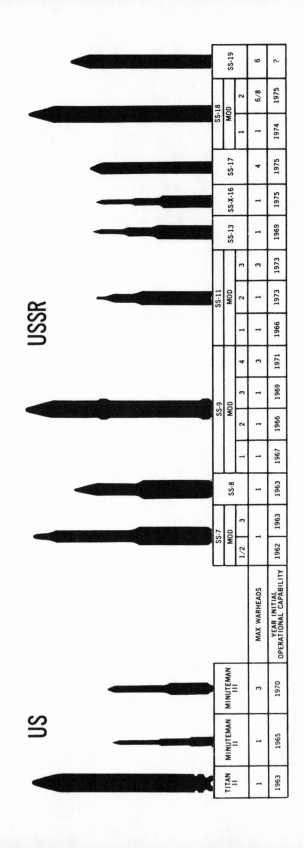

US

	TITAN II	MINUTEMAN II	MINUTEMAN III
MAX WARHEADS	1	1	3
YEAR INITIAL OPERATIONAL CAPABILITY	1963	1965	1970

USSR

	SS-7		SS-8	SS-9				SS-11			SS-13	SS-X-16	SS-17	SS-18		SS-19
MOD	1/2	3		1	2	3	4	1	2	3				1	MOD 2	
MAX WARHEADS	1	3	1	1	1	1	3	1	1	3	1	1	4	1	6/8	6
YEAR INITIAL OPERATIONAL CAPABILITY	1962	1963	1963	1967	1966	1969	1971	1966	1973	1973	1969	1975	1975	1974	1975	?

orbital (FOBS) mode. There has been no known test of this system since August of 1971, and we entertain considerable uncertainty as to its precise capabilities and the extent of its deployment. Nonetheless, we do not believe it has been deployed to any of the regular SS-9 operational complexes.

MOD 4 flight tests resumed in 1973. None were detected in 1974. There is no known reason for the 1973 resumption of testing, but the absence of any test in 1974 suggests either that the 1973 effort achieved some research and development objectives or that the testing supported a new program which, for other reasons, was discontinued.

There were originally 288 SS-9s deployed. Some of these silos already have been converted to launchers for more advanced missiles and other silos are now undergoing conversion.

SS-11

The two-stage SS-11, operational since 1966, remains the most extensively deployed Soviet ICBM. It has been subjected to extensive troop testing, including over 100 launches from operational silos. There are three versions of this liquid-propelled weapon, none of which employs a sufficient combination of accuracy and yield to constitute an effective threat to either Minuteman or any other hard target.

Lack of identifiable operational testing led us to believe that the MOD 2 program had been terminated. Recent firings suggest crew training, and indicate that deployment possibly may have been initiated. Like the MOD 1, this is a single-warhead weapon, but it also has been tested with penetration aids designed to assist the penetration of an anti-ballistic missile (ABM) system. The MOD 3 has three MRV warheads. We believe that MOD 3s already have been deployed in the silos under construction at the time the Interim Agreement was signed. The remainder of the force is composed of MOD 1s.

SS-13

The last of the previously displayed Soviet missiles shown on Chart 1 is the SS-13. This missile has been operational since 1969 and utilizes a solid propellant. Sixty of these missiles currently are deployed. It is estimated that it will be replaced by the SS-X-16, a weapon much more accurate than the current system.

SS-X-16

The SS-X-16 utilizes a solid propellant. Apparently, there had been some difficulty with this missile. It is believed now that the difficulties have been overcome. In December 1974, two SS-X-16s were launched to the Pacific test range—4,200 nautical miles.

The SS-X-16, with much greater throwweight than the SS-13 and an advanced navigation guidance system, has a post-boost vehicle traditionally associated with dispensing MIRVs, but to date has been tested only with a single warhead. It is expected to replace the SS-13. The single warhead version probably may be operational this year. A MIRV version also may be deployed, but not until at least a year after testing begins. The anticipated SAL (Strategic Arms Limitations) undertakings may constrain the MIRVing of this missile.

There is, however, a more serious question associated with the SS-X-16. Circumstantial evidence continues to indicate that this weapon is being developed as a land-based mobile system. Its deployment is probably dependent on the outcome of the more comprehensive agreement under negotiation, as well as on successful development. Senior officers of the Soviet Strategic Rocket Force have spoken constantly of their mobile and invulnerable force; however, throughout the negotiations leading to the Interim Agreement, the Soviet Union rejected US efforts to ban deployment of land-mobile strategic offensive systems. Since we were unable to achieve any constraint on such systems, the United States delegation stated unilaterally that we "would consider the deployment of operational land-mobile ICBM launchers during the period of the Interim Agreement as inconsistent with the objectives of that Agreement."

It is against this background that the evidence of development and/or deployment should be examined.

Soviet strategic policy is shaped by a maze of complex considerations. There are many competing factors which will determine whether a mobile system will be deployed. Those favoring deployment include: increased survivability; projection of an image of Soviet strength; a hedge against lapse of the Interim Agreement; institutional momentum and sunk costs; and a bargaining chip in future negotiations. The Vladivostok framework will permit the deployment of ground-mobile ICBMs, but they will be included in the 2,400 launcher cap. Reliability, accuracy, and availability are reduced considerably by the problems inherent in mobility, while operating costs, including maintenance, security, and positive control, are substantially higher than those associated with fixed deployment.

SS-17

This is a liquid-propellant ICBM. The system employs a sabot "cold"-launch technique with main engine ignition outside of the silo.

We believe that the missile dispenses four MIRV warheads from a post-boost vehicle. It is estimated that the missile will become operational in 1975.

SS-18

The SS-18 is a large, liquid-propellant, "cold"-launch ICBM comparable in volume to the SS-9. We have identified two variants of this missile. The over 5,500-nautical mile MOD 1 system employs a sophisticated version of the traditional Soviet "fly-the-wire" control system with an on-board digital computer. This missile, with much greater destructive power than Titan and improved accuracy, is capable of destroying any known fixed target. This variant is now operational, while the MOD 2 test program is proceeding at a somewhat slower pace. The MIRVed version has dispensed at least six RVs and is believed capable of deploying as many as eight warheads to a range of 5,500 nautical miles. This missile could be operational in 1975.

SS-19

The SS-19 is a "hot"-launched, liquid-propellant missile, which was first tested in April 1973. Its throwweight is three to four times that of the SS-11, and it is much larger in volume. Its guidance system combines navigation with a refinement of traditional Soviet "fly-the-wire" guidance technique. An on-board computer determines deviation from the preprogrammed course, and directs correction to that course or plots a new course to the target depending on the attendant circumstances. It is believed that this missile is capable of delivering, at a range of 5,000 nautical miles, six MIRVed warheads. The SS-19 now may be starting to be deployed in operational silos.

It was reported last year that there was some question as to whether both the SS-17 and the SS-19 were to be deployed; that it appeared the "17" was the most advanced vehicle; and that neither would be operational prior to 1975. It now appears that we again underestimated the scope and the intensity of the Soviet program.

Follow-On Systems

There are indications from diverse sources which, in combination, lead to the conclusion that the USSR is not completely satisfied despite the significant improvements in force effectiveness displayed by the four new systems. It appears that their R&D effort has momentum which will continue.

Launcher Inventory

Projected on Chart 2 are our latest estimates of US-USSR ICBM forces through mid-1975.

US AND USSR ICBM LAUNCHERS
(INVENTORY)

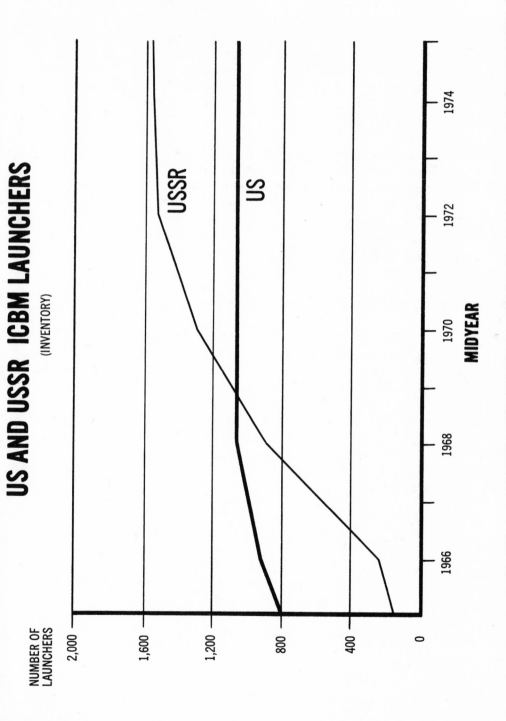

In this connection, it is essential that a very fundamental premise be understood. This chart and all those that follow are based upon the assumption that the relevant numerical limitations imposed by the Interim Agreement will remain in effect through October 1977, and that the 2,400 and 1,320 Vladivostok numbers will be implemented.

This chart and the quantitative ones that follow were developed in order to facilitate measuring the strategic balance. There is a considerable amount of professional judgment involved in both the measurement and the selection of criteria to be measured. I would urge in your consideration of the evidence that weight be given to each element, but that no single element be considered in isolation from the other qualitative and quantitative measures of the balance.

We estimate that the USSR at mid-1975 will have 1,591 ICBM launchers.

Whatever the underlying motivation, it does not appear that they expect negotiations to negate their near-term deployment plans. It is our best estimate that the demonstrated rapid modernization of the USSR's ICBM force will continue.

With regard to US ICBMs, I have no dramatic program to present. The Secretary already has described our deliberate and modest force improvement proposals. No new ICBM system is currently under engineering development, although we are seeking to develop the technology which will allow us to improve our posture in a timely fashion if we are unable by negotiations to arrest the strong Soviet underlying momentum short of significant strategic superiority. To this end, we are exploring the opportunity to increase the yield of the Minuteman-III warhead. Likewise, we are seeking to develop the technology necessary to increase the number of warheads on Minuteman-III. Furthermore, we expect to continue to search for software and other improvements which further will mature the Minuteman guidance system and improve the system's accuracy. We also are looking at terminally-guided maneuvering reentry vehicles (MaRV) for possible deployment with ICBMs and SLBMs.

As you will recall, the advanced ICBM technology program was converted in FY 1974 to an integrated development program, combining system concept studies and technology developments, to provide the basis for a new ICBM should such a vehicle become necessary. The program goals are to enlarge its throwweight over that of Minuteman and to increase its survivability through further hardening or by making the system ground- or air-mobile.

The last Minuteman-I has been deactivated. Minuteman-IIs are being replaced by Minuteman-IIIs to reach a force mix of 450 Minuteman-IIs, 550 Minuteman-IIIs, and 54 Titan-IIs.

In FY 1976, we plan to continue the advanced technology approach we have been pursuing with the M-X Advanced ICBM. This initiative will provide the necessary hedge against the unknowns in the strategic environment of the mid-1980s. A decision to enter engineering development of, or to deploy, the M-X Advanced ICBM is several years away; and it will be based upon a continuing assessment of both SALT progress and the state of Soviet military developments.

US and USSR SLBM Forces

Prior to discussing the relative balance of these forces, I should like again to refer to the basic provisions of the Interim Agreement pertaining to SLBMs and ballistic missile submarines.

The Agreement limits SLBM launchers and modern ballistic missiles to the number operational and under construction on 26 May 1972. On that date, the US construction program had terminated and we operated 41 SSBNs, each with 16 launch tubes, for a total of 656 launchers. The parties were, however, unable to agree as to the number the USSR would be permitted under this formula. Due to this uncertainty, it was necessary to conclude a Protocol establishing a negotiated artificial ceiling. It was agreed that the USSR "had" 740 ballistic missile launchers on nuclear-powered submarines operational or under construction as of 26 May 1972.

Also, the Agreement permitted additions to each SLBM/SSBN force subject to two constraints. First, the quantitative growth of the force was conditioned upon dismantling (a) an equal number of ICBM launchers initially deployed prior to 1964 (SS-7s and SS-8s, Titans); (b) SLBM launchers on older nuclear-powered submarines (Hotel and Yankee, Polaris/Poseidon); or (c) "modern" SLBM launchers on any type submarine. Second, there was an absolute upper limit of 62 modern ballistic missile submarines and 950 SLBMs for the USSR and corresponding numbers of 44 and 710 for the United States. Under the Vladivostok understanding, these numbers remain valid only through October 1977, when they will be subsumed within the 2,400 total strategic vehicle and 1,320 MIRV limitations, and will no longer operate as submarine/SLBM limits.

Chart 3 provides a comparison of US and USSR SLBMs. Even though the Trident C-4 is still not operational, I have included it because of its continued importance to the future of the strategic balance.

SS-N-5

The SS-N-5 first entered the Soviet force in 1963. It has a relatively short range (700 nautical miles). Nonetheless, because of the warhead size, it is an effective weapon against soft targets such as centers of mass population. There are currently 24 SAL-accountable operational launchers for these missiles; however, we expect that they all will be deleted from the inventory as a result of the continuing modernization momentum.[47]

SS-N-6

The SS-N-6 first entered the Soviet naval inventory in 1968, and at present, is the most widely deployed Soviet submarine-launched weapons system. As indicated, it has three separate operational var-

---

[47] These 24 SS-N-5 missiles are in light Hotel-class nuclear-propelled submarines; it is assumed that the ninth submarine of this class is employed in research and development activities, and may no longer be a deployable SLBM craft.

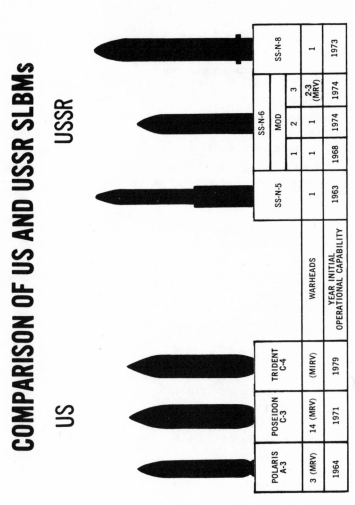

CHART NO. 3

COMPARISON OF US AND USSR SLBMs

US

	POLARIS A-3	POSEIDON C-3	TRIDENT C-4
WARHEADS	3 (MRV)	14 (MRV)	(MIRV)
YEAR INITIAL OPERATIONAL CAPABILITY	1964	1971	1979

USSR

	SS-N-5	SS-N-6 MOD 1	SS-N-6 MOD 2	SS-N-6 MOD 3	SS-N-8
WARHEADS	1	1	1	2-3 (MRV)	1
YEAR INITIAL OPERATIONAL CAPABILITY	1963	1968	1974	1974	1973

iants, and we estimate that they are relatively interchangeable. All are liquid-fueled. The MOD 1 is a single-warhead weapon with a range of 1,300 nautical miles. It is expected that the SS-N-6 system will be phased out as the modernization momentum continues.

In October 1972, flight testing began on a modified version of the SS-N-6. This system, the MOD 2, reached an IOC (Initial Operational Capability) in 1974. The most significant modification was in the propulsion system, resulting in a 300-nautical mile increase in range to 1,600 nautical miles. We believe that the SS-N-6 is now capable of reaching any target in the United States from the 100-fathom curve off the coasts of the United States. This missile also is expected to be withdrawn in favor of more effective systems.

The SS-N-6 MOD 3 represents a further development in Soviet missile technology. This 1,600-nautical mile weapon carries MRVs and probably reached IOC in 1974. These warheads are not independently targeted. The combination of yield and accuracy for all versions of the SS-N-6 limits its effectiveness to soft targets.

We believe that the current level of 544 launchers for this missile, some of which are MRVs, will remain in the Soviet inventory until a new SS-N-6-sized missile begins to enter the inventory.

SS-N-8

The SS-N-8 has a much greater volume than the SS-N-6, and reached IOC in 1973. It is a liquid-propelled missile capable of delivering a single warhead to a range of 4,200 nautical miles. This weapon remains unique in two particulars. It exceeds, by at least 1,600 nautical miles, the range of any other SLBM currently deployed by either the USSR or the United States.

US SLBMs

The older, single warhead Polaris A-2 missile now has been phased out of our deployed inventory completely. Only the Polaris A-3 (three MRVs) and the MIRVed Poseidon C-3 missiles are currently at sea. Both are two-stage, solid-propellant, inertially-guided missiles.

The Trident C-4 missile has been designed with range characteristics which will permit basing in the United States without sacrifice of alert rate, and which will permit an operating area increase of at least four times that which we currently enjoy. We are, however, asking to continue a small parallel advanced development effort to provide an option for the early 1980s for major accuracy improvement, as well as the advanced development of an evading reentry vehicle (MaRV), as a hedge against Soviet actions to upgrade their SAMs to ABM capability.

The IOC of the new missile is planned for late 1977 and will coincide with the completion of the first Trident submarine. It is on schedule. As you will recall, it is virtually interchangeable with the Poseidon C-3, and will be backfitted into ten such submarines beginning in 1979.

Turning now to the launch platforms for these missiles, Chart 4 displays the four operational Soviet submarine-launched ballistic missile platforms and the US Polaris/Poseidon submarine.

USSR Submarines

Golf

The Golf is a diesel-powered submarine and represents the first Soviet submarine class to have been built from the keel up to launch ballistic missiles. The lead ship was completed in 1958 and became operational in 1960. The 20 operational Golf submarines are not counted in the SAL limits. The class is included here only in the interest of completeness.

Hotel

Nine Hotel-class submarines originally were built. This submarine is a nuclear-powered vessel capable of firing three SS-N-5 missiles. We believe eight such units are now operational.

OPERATIONAL BALLISTIC MISSILE SUBMARINES

		YEAR OPERATIONAL	PROPULSION	MISSILE	
USSR					
D CLASS	450 FT	1973	NUCLEAR	12	SS-N-8
Y CLASS	425 FT	1968	NUCLEAR	16	SS-N-6
G CLASS	380 FT	1960	NUCLEAR	3	SS-N-5
H CLASS	320 FT	1960	DIESEL	3	SS-N-4/5
US					
POLARIS	382 AND 410 FT	1960	NUCLEAR	16	A-3
POSEIDON	425 FT	1971	NUCLEAR	16	C-3

Yankee

This 428-foot class is similar in concept, size, and layout to the United States Lafayette-class SSBN. Missile tubes sized for the SS-N-6 are arranged in two rows of eight. The lead ship reached IOC in 1968.

There is reason to believe that production of the Yankee has terminated. These 34 units, with their 544 launch tubes, are expected to constitute the bulk of the Soviet force for some years to come.

Delta

The latest Soviet SSBN to be deployed is the 450-foot Delta, which began patrol in mid-1974. This submarine has 12 launch tubes capable of handling the SS-N-8.

Lengthened Delta-Class Submarines

The Soviet Union has announced that it intends to build to the full extent of the Interim Agreement limits. We believe that they will build a force close to the 62 modern submarines and the 950 SLBMs allowed. In order to do so, at a reasonable cost, a larger launch vehicle for the SS-N-8 is required. Further, there is evidence that the USSR soon will launch the first of a lengthened version of the Delta—a "super" Delta. This added length will permit the installation of more launch tubes than the standard Delta.

US SSBNs

The two lead Polaris classes of five ships each, because of their size, cannot be converted to either the Poseidon C-3 or the Trident C-4 missile. These ships average 14 years old. The other class is being converted to Poseidon C-3 configurations. All 31 vessels will be converted by early FY 1978.

The Trident submarine is designed to employ 24 missile tubes, and yet, will be faster and quieter than the Poseidon. By the end of 1978, we hope to have Trident operational.

Prior to summarizing the quantitative SLBM balance and estimating the future forces, it is important to note one further qualitative factor bearing on the relative effectiveness of the forces. The readiness of a force, particularly the SLBM force, is related clearly to the capability to maintain the material condition of individual submarines at an acceptable level by regular and timely overhaul. The average period for overhauling a US nuclear submarine is much less than in the USSR.

The current projections of US and USSR SLBM launchers operational or on sea trials are shown on Chart 5. SLBMs on sea trials are included because of the structure of the Interim Agreement—the dismantlement of older systems must be initiated when sea trials begin for any new SLBMs.

We estimate that by mid-1975, the Soviet Union will have a total of 700 missile launchers on 52 nuclear-powered submarines. The US force will be composed of 656 missiles on 41 SSBNs.

US and USSR Strategic Bomber Forces

Chart 6 shows US and USSR Strategic Bomber Forces projected through mid-1975.

US Bombers

More than a decade ago, we identified the requirement to modernize the manned bomber portion of our strategic deterrent forces. The B-1 has been designed as an extremely versatile aircraft capable of performing in hostile environments with a high degree of safety and mission success probability. Its variable-geometry (swing) wing will permit it to use shorter runways and to maximize performance at altitude and speed extremes. The radar cross-section has been reduced greatly over the B-52. It will get into the air in far less time than is required by the B-52, and will carry about twice the weapons load over the same intercontinental distances. Armament planned for the B-1 includes the SRAM, both nuclear and conventional bombs,

US AND USSR SLBM LAUNCHERS

(INVENTORY)

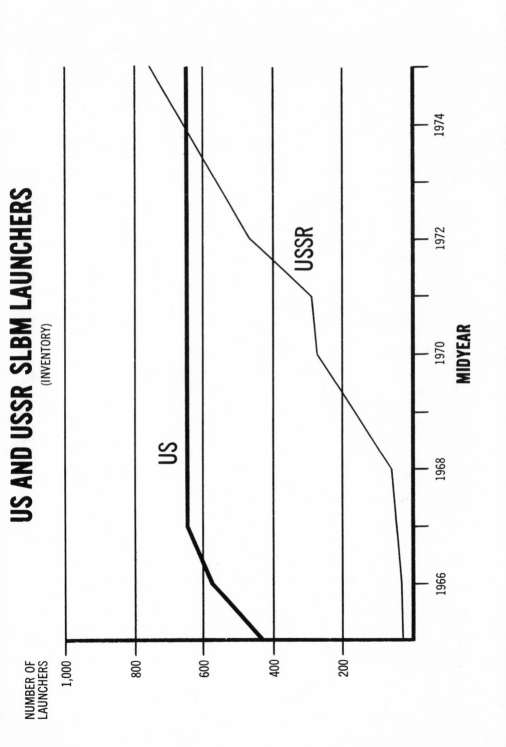

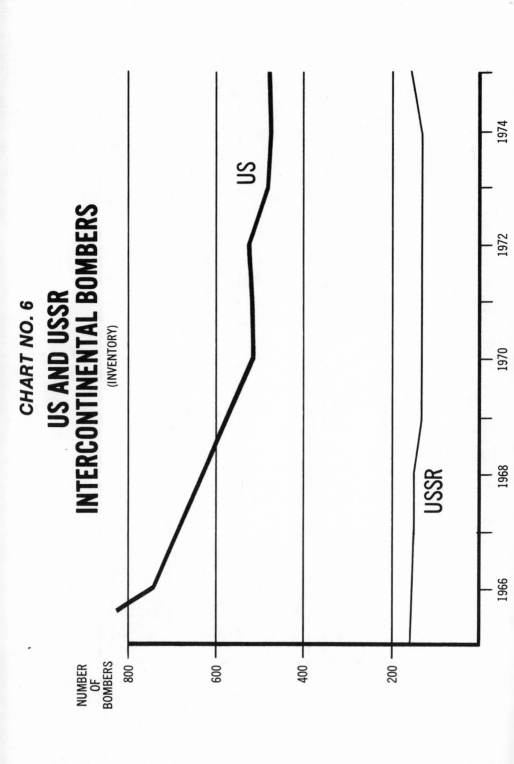

CHART NO. 6

US AND USSR
INTERCONTINENTAL BOMBERS
(INVENTORY)

NUMBER
OF
BOMBERS

800

600

400

200

US

USSR

1966   1968   1970   1972   1974

and special electronic countermeasures designed to assist in the penetration of the most sophisticated defenses we can project into the 21st century.

The B-1 began flight testing late last December. A production decision will be made in late 1976 subsequent to detailed performance evaluation of the three prototype aircraft now scheduled for construction. The B-1 will provide the nation with capabilities far beyond those currently provided by the B-52 and FB-111. It also will have important qualitative advantages over the impressive capabilities of the Backfire, which the USSR has deployed recently. I consider the capability of the B-1 as a virtually indispensable element of our deterrent force.

Until the 1980s, when the B-1 would enter the inventory in significant numbers, the B-52 and the FB-111 will continue to constitute the US intercontinental bomber force. The structural modification program for the B-52Ds in order to maintain this force level is on schedule. Wing strength testing began in October 1974. By September 1976, we expect to have completed the required partial reskinning of the wing and fuselage.

USSR Bombers

The new Soviet variable-geometry wing bomber, Backfire—under testing since late 1969—is now entering the operational inventory. With inflight refueling and staged from Arctic bases, Backfire could cover virtually all of the United States on two-way subsonic missions with limited low-level penetration. Staging from the Chukotsk Peninsula, the unrefueled radius would cover the western United States in an arc generally extending from the western US-Mexican border to the eastern tip of Lake Superior. On one-way missions, recovering in friendly or neutral territory, the Backfire is capable of delivering weapons anywhere in the United States without refueling. Carrying ASMs (air-to-surface missiles) the Backfire would have somewhat reduced capabilities, but the potential range of the ASM would produce comparable target coverage. Tanker support would be required for intercontinental missions involving supersonic dash or extended low-altitude operations. In this connection, it should be recalled that while some 50 of the Bison aircraft are tankers, the other bombers could be converted eventually to tankers. Bison probably could refuel Backfire, and all the Backfires produced are believed to have a refueling probe. Further, there is some evidence that the Soviet Union is developing a tanker variant of the Il-76 Candid jet transport.

The Backfire is a versatile, multipurpose aircraft capable of performing nuclear strike, conventional attack, anti-ship, reconnaissance, and electronic warfare missions. It has extensive capabilities for various types of peripheral missions against NATO Europe and China. Unrefueled, it probably is best suited for that role. Its intercontinental capabilities cannot be prudently ignored, particularly in the face of thinning US air defenses.

This chart reflects only long-range bombers. Intermediate-range bombers are omitted from the force displayed here, notwithstanding the fact that some of them have a potential intercontinental strike capability if Arctic staging and one-way flight profiles are used. We do not know precisely how the Soviet planner intends to utilize the Backfire weapons system. Evidence derived from basing, operational activities, and training patterns ultimately will answer this question. This is an excellent example of why I believe we must deal realistically with demonstrated capabilities, not perceived intentions. The Soviet General Staff could change the Backfire mission in a matter of hours, if not minutes; but preparing a defense against such an increased threat could require years.

Our ability to detect Soviet aircraft at the developmental stage prior to the rollout of a new prototype is limited. Continued development of Backfire indicates a continuing interest in the bomber as a strategic weapon system.

The Backfire, an improved version thereof, or a new bomber with increased range and payload probably would satisfy new bomber requirements through the 1980s. We have no evidence of such a new system. The design of any new Soviet bomber would be tailored to the Soviet Union's perception of its requirements. If the USSR decides to develop a new long-range bomber, we would expect to become aware of its existence a number of years prior to its IOC.

USSR Air-to-Surface Missiles

In the event of a strategic attack against the United States, we believe the USSR would employ stockpiled nuclear bombs with a wide range of yields. In addition, the Bear-B and -C carry the large AS-3 Kangaroo air-to-surface guided missile. We believe that an air-to-surface missile is being developed for the Backfire.

US Air-to-Surface Weapons

On the US side, a new bomb is now in engineering development. A mixed air-launched cruise missile/SRAM force will complicate Soviet defensive planning, extend bomber range, and provide increased coverage for lower priority undefended targets. Furthermore, the decision to equip B-52s with Harpoon anti-ship missiles will add to the ability of strategic aircraft to support interdependently the sea surveillance mission.

US and USSR Strategic Offensive Balance

Quantitative measures are, however, only one segment of the equation, and caution is required in order to avoid overreliance on any single factor or combination of such factors in making the judgments necessary to a full understanding of the relative power of the United States and our ability to deter attack by the USSR. Alert rate, command, control, communications, attack warning, survivability, systems reliability, range, penetration capability, and accuracy are among the many factors not subject to reasonable quantification which play a very significant role in assessing balance. I have retained the four general measures—delivery vehicles, megatons, warheads, and throwweight/payload—which have become traditional in this presentation. Only those weapons readily available for employment are displayed.

Chart 7 reflects the fact that the USSR has surpassed us in the number of delivery vehicles.

The principal significance of this small lead is in historical perspective. Less than a decade ago, the United States enjoyed a five-to-one lead. Balanced bomber construction, the restraints on new construction imposed by the Interim Agreement, and the reduced availability resulting from the intensive silo modernization program now under way in the USSR should ensure that the Soviet lead is not widened substantially over the period of this report.

Strategic offensive megatonnage is a very gross measure of the balance. The greater the Soviet effort to modernize and to MIRV, the more rapidly its total megatonnage will fall. This is also the explanation for the rapid reduction in total US megatonnage from 1970 to date.

The number of strategic warheads and bombs is a very significant measure of the balance. Mr. Brezhnev has been quoted as stating: "Warheads—not launchers—kill." This fact adds a degree of importance to the relative number of warheads. Last year, it was believed that even if the Soviet Union pursued a program of rapid modernization, our substantial lead could be "diminished but not eliminated." It is now clear that this judgment understated both the breadth and intensity of the Soviet effort to surpass the United States in this measure of the strategic balance.

If the Soviet Union continues its present rapid modernization effort, the substantial US advantage will be lost by mid-1979. Unless we initiate new programs or restrain this massive Soviet growth by the ongoing arms control negotiations, we reasonably may expect the Soviet Union to dominate this measure of the balance. If, as Secretary Schlesinger has indicated, they are attempting to develop a hard-target kill capability, a numerical advantage of even 1,000 warheads has considerable strategic significance.

I suggest that the continual growth of Soviet throwweight is an important consideration. The weight of that part of the missile above the last boost stage and representative loadings of aircraft are re-

US AND USSR OPERATIONAL STRATEGIC OFFENSIVE DELIVERY VEHICLES

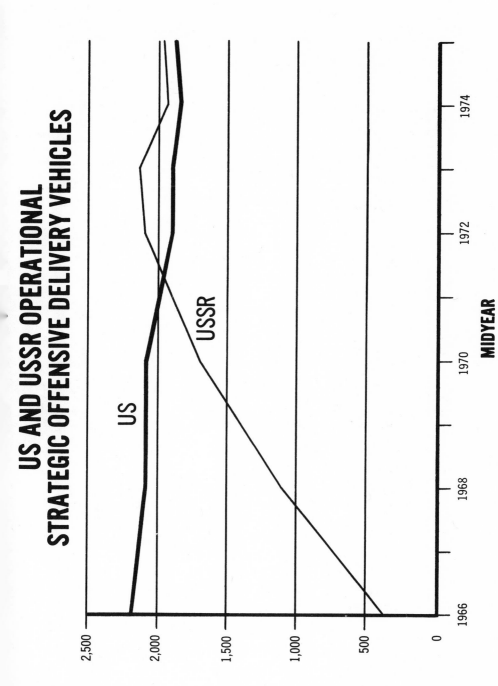

US

USSR

MIDYEAR

1966   1968   1970   1972   1974

0   500   1,000   1,500   2,000   2,500

ferred to as throwweight and payload. Notwithstanding a two-to-one advantage, the USSR appears to be building an even greater advantage. It may be that this superiority will exceed even three to one. In spite of the fact that we believe that the heavy SS-7s and SS-8s may be replaced by appreciably lighter SLBMs, Soviet throwweight could continue to grow as each new system deploys greater throwweight than the system it is replacing. The United States is expected to offset this advantage somewhat by continuing to retain a substantial lead in bomber payload. It is essential that we continue research and development activities I have noted previously so that we retain the option of deploying a missile with increased throwweight in the event such deployment becomes necessary in order to preserve a viable deterrent.

US and USSR Strategic Defense Forces

The strategic equation places great stress on the ordinary meanings attributed to the terms "offense" and "defense." Either type force can be used for aggression or protection. Thus, it is clear that if a nation has the ability to destroy a given percentage of a potential adversary's force by a preemptive strike and is able to defend against the remainder, the capability of launching an effective disarming first strike has been achieved. In this arena, a potential adversary's defensive effort must be viewed in the same context as his attack capability if a viable deterrent is to be maintained.

Prior to discussing the relationship between the US and USSR defensive forces, it is again necessary to set the stage in terms of the results of agreements on limiting strategic arms. The 1972 ABM Treaty limits each party to a relatively small and equal ABM force—originally two sites each of no more than 100 launchers and 100 missiles and a controlled number of associated radars. One site may be centered on the national capital, and the other on ICBM silos. The parties also undertook not to develop, test, or deploy ABM systems or components which are sea-based, air-based, space-based, or mobile land-based. On July 3, 1974, we signed, in Moscow, a protocol to the ABM Treaty which, upon ratification, will further limit the USSR and the United States to only one such ABM site. Each party, after properly notifying the other, will have the right to dismantle or destroy its current site and to deploy ABMs otherwise permitted in the alternate area. This site exchange may take place during the first year of successive five-year intervals beginning in October 1977, but this option may be exercised only once.

ABM

The Moscow ABM system consists of battle management radars, engagement radars, and Galosh missile launchers. Eight complexes were originally under construction, but only four with 64 missile launchers have been completed. Each operational complex consists of two large target-tracking radars, four smaller or interceptor guidance and tracking radars, and 16 missile launchers.

This system, which we have designated ABM-1B, includes target acquisition and tracking radars such as Dog House, Chekhov, and Hen House. It provides little defense against a large-scale or penetration-aided attack. It would, however, provide a credible defense of Moscow and a large portion of Soviet ICBM silos against a small, accidental, or unauthorized attack.

The US Army has completed the Safeguard test program which began at Kwajalein Island in 1970. By April 1975, we expect to reach IOC at the Grand Forks site. The scheduled Equipment Readiness Date of October 1, 1974 was met; and by October 1975, we expect to have a full operational capability with Spartan long-range and short-range Sprint missile interceptors, a Perimeter Acquisition Radar for acquisition at long range, a Missile Site Radar for accurate tracking and interceptor guidance, and a Ballistic Missile Defense Center.

We thus will be able, within the capabilities afforded by Spartan and Sprint missile interceptors, to provide a terminal defense of a portion of the Grand Forks Minuteman field and a limited area defense against accidental/unauthorized launches in the Colorado/Dakotas region covered by the Spartan "footprint." After all subsystems are interfaced and brought to full operational condition, we will be able to validate the total spectrum of the subsystem design, including compatibility with the national command and control structure.

The USSR is pursuing vigorously the development of advanced technology applicable to its ABM force.

I do not believe that the USSR has deployed its extensive network to provide ABM defense, nor do I believe that it is currently suitable for that role. I remain convinced that we would be able to detect any program designed to upgrade SAMs to an effective ABM capability, but we must be alert to that possibility.

During the latter part of this decade, the Soviet Union may deploy follow-on systems around Moscow to the level permitted by the ABM treaty.

The Site Defense Program is the US effort to maintain an equivalent capability. It provides a hedge to deploy a credible ABM defense for Minuteman to counter the Soviet capability to threaten Minuteman survivability in the 1980s, if follow-on negotiations do not otherwise insure the survivability of a sufficient strategic retaliatory force. We are emphasizing the development of improved subsystems and components, rather than "prototype demonstration," in accordance with guidance of the Congress. In the Advanced Technology Program, we are pursuing a vigorous research effort embracing technology applicable to all components and functions of ballistic missile defense, which must be understood to maintain our technological lead. The objectives of the effort are to provide an advanced technology foundation for future systems, to avoid technological surprise, and to assist in the design and evaluation of US strategic offensive systems.

Air Defense

The Soviet Union's strategic air defense is by far the most extensive and expensive in the world. It operates over 4,000 radars located at early warning and ground control intercept (EW/GCI) radar sites, over 2,600 fighter interceptors, and about 12,000 strategic surface-to-air missiles (SAMs) on launchers.

Chart 8 displays the numerical imbalance in the current force structure. However, it must be remembered that many of the currently-deployed Soviet air defense systems were designed originally to counter the medium-to-high altitude bomber and stand-off missile threats represented by the B-70 and the evolving technology of the late 1950s and early 1960s. The force, nonetheless, displays significant capabilities.

Interceptors

The right side of the chart compares US and USSR home defense interceptors projected through mid-1975. The Soviet deployment levels have continued their steady decline (about 100 aircraft per year) which began in 1964, but the overall capability of the force continues to mount. Older, largely gun-armed interceptors, such as Fresco MiG-17 and Farmer MiG-19, are being replaced by more sophisticated, all-weather interceptors, such as the Foxbat MiG-25 and Flagon-E Su-15. The Flagon-E entered operational service just over a year ago. It employs a new and more powerful propulsion system, which increases both speed and range, and improved avionics in addition to advanced air-to-air missiles. It appears that the Flogger MiG-23, a single-engine variable-geometry wing fighter, armed with four air-to-air missiles and an additional gun, also is being prepared for an air defeense role.

We expect the Soviet Union to deploy in the 1977-80 timeframe a new interceptor. In the interim, the USSR is expected to continue widening the capabilities of the interceptor force by emphasizing the modification of existing aircraft rather than introducing entirely new systems. The fundamental constraint on Soviet interceptor effectiveness against low-altitude bombers is that they have not demonstrated the capability of developing a radar capable of detecting and tracking from high altitude a bomber at low altitude against a background of signals reflecting from the ground.

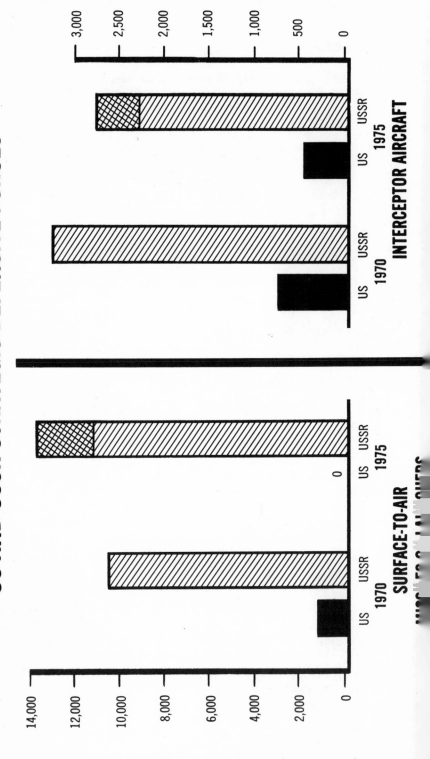

CHART NO. 8

US AND USSR STRATEGIC DEFENSIVE FORCES

The mid-1975 US operational interceptor force will be composed of 116 F-101s, 56 F-102s, and 233 F-106s. All these interceptors entered the inventory in the 1950s. This force will, however, be 65 percent Air National Guard. By mid-1980, the force will be reduced to 122 active and 90 Air National Guard F-106s. General purpose augmentation aircraft stationed in the United States, of course, will be available to assist in the air defense mission prior to their deployment to overseas locations.

Shown on the left side of Chart 8 are US and USSR home defense SAM forces. The US strategic SAM force was totally deactivated in 1974. There was a slight increase in the Soviet number in 1974.

Soviet Strategic SAM Force

This force is composed of four systems. The SA-1 Guild is a liquid-propelled missile first deployed in 1954. We estimate that the mid-1975 level of sites will decrease gradually as Soviet modernization increases.

The SA-2 Guideline is the command-guided, high-altitude missile which the North Vietnamese employed with a reasonable degree of effectiveness during Linebacker-II (the intensive air attacks against North Vietnam in December 1972). This system, which was first introduced in 1958, like virtually all Soviet strategic SAM systems, has been modernized during its lifetime with new versions, increasing its range and improving its performance at low altitudes. Some of the guidance systems have been modified with optics, thus providing improved low-altitude capabilities. We estimate that the SA-2 force will continue to decline.

The SA-3 Goa is a road-transportable, solid-propelled medium- and low-altitude, command-guided missile employed in both the point defense and barrier role. This system, first introduced in early 1961, is capable of intercepting attacking aircraft at low altitudes within a limited range of the launch site. We estimate that the mid-1975 level of sites will increase.

The latest Soviet strategic SAM system is the SA-5 Gammon, which was initially operational in 1967. It provides point defense for certain vital areas of strategic importance.

Although not a strategic system, the highly mobile SA-6, employed with notable effectiveness in the recent Middle East hostilities, has impressive capabilities, particularly in dealing with low-altitude attacks.

Despite the size of the Soviet air defense force and the projected improvements, there exists major weakness in low-altitude defense against penetrating bombers and in defense against the US Short-Range Attack Missile (SRAM). This will require the USSR to attempt to attack and destroy the SRAM carriers as early as possible. Early detection is indispensable to this effort.

The Moss aircraft still provides the USSR with its limited Airborne Controlled Intercept (ACI) capability. The aircraft has worked in overwater exercises, but is unequal to the more challenging overland task. If the USSR intends to improve its air defense, a new airborne warning and control aircraft system, a better radar network for GCI, and better airborne radars probably will be required. There is as yet no evidence that the Soviet Union is developing an Airborne Warning and Control System (AWACS) capable of detecting and tracking aircraft at low altitudes over land.

Last year, the Secretary of Defense announced a decision to readjust the primary air defense mission to encompass surveillance; peacetime control of US airspace; and warning of a bomber, missile, or space attack. This decision was forced by tight budget constraints and the fact that without effective ABM defenses, air defenses are of limited value against potential aggressors armed with strategic missiles.

I would be less than candid if I were to leave the impression that there were no risks in this phased-down program. By mid-1976, our limited interceptor force will average about 18 years of age. The majority of the general purpose fighters are committed to other contingency plans and may not be available for air defense. We will be without terminal defense of high-value urban/industrial areas against either a bomber or cruise missile attack. It is, therefore, essential that the Congress provide funds to preserve the option of deploying on a timely basis a new interceptor (e.g., F-15 or F-14), a new SAM system (e.g., SAM-D), and AWACS for strategic defense should some significant change in the strategic structure become necessary in the future. These programs now are being provided for the general purpose forces, and they deserve consideration in the context of both that mission and the defense of the United States in time of crisis. They will make it possible to provide a pool of strategic and general prupose tri-service assets from which resources could be drawn to provide air defense for threatened areas overseas as well as in the United States.

PRC Strategic Forces

The dramatically increasing prominence of the People's Republic of China in foreign policy calculations is only partially reflected in its military program. There is a steady, almost painstaking quality about this relatively small, but carefully conceived, strategic program. A modest, but credible, nuclear retaliatory capability against the USSR has been achieved, and this undoubtedly has influenced the decision to move ahead slowly, but deliberately, with the task of increasing the effectiveness of PRC nuclear forces. Emphasis is clearly on programs with long-range implications, such as the construction of two of the world's most modern shipyards at Hu-lu-tao and Kuang-chi; impressive new facilities for producing large quantities of nuclear materials; solid propellant missiles; and R&D initiatives addressing advanced airframes and sophisticated engines. The temptation to yield to programs which would provide a more immediate strategic posture and perception of growing strength apparently has been resisted.

MRBM Force

This force is composed of a single-stage, liquid-propellant, transportable system developed from Soviet models. The estimated range is about 600 nautical miles. It can reach targets in the eastern USSR, peripheral nations, and some US bases in the Far East. It is an obsolescent and cumbersome missile system with slow reaction time.

IRBM

This single-stage, liquid-propellant ballistic missile presently is deployed at permanent sites. Its range is about 1,500 nautical miles. During the past year, deployment of this system continued at a measured, deliberate rate.

Limited Range ICBM

We now estimate that a limited range system could become operational during 1975. The program, however, continues to be a major enigma in the PRC's strategic weapons effort. When it reaches IOC, the PRC will have a limited capability to cover targets in the European USSR—possibly including Moscow. The PRC may consider the creation of such a capability sufficient justification for deploying only a few of these largely untested missiles. The reasons behind this decision, of course, are unknown, but could include political, budgetary, and strategic factors.

ICBM

This is a large ICBM in the same class as the US Titan and the Soviet SS-9. It could have a range of about 7,000 nautical miles.

Full flight-testing of this missile will require launches to a broad ocean impact area, probably in the Pacific, but possibly into the Indian Ocean. Analysis of such launches will provide much more data about characteristics of the system than we now have.

The PRC has made a substantial investment over the past 15 years in research, developmental testing, and production facilities for both liquid and solid-propellant missile systems. All current operational Chinese ballistic missile systems use liquid propellants. The PRC's continuing interest in facilities capable of developing and producing solid-propellant rocket motors of various sizes up through intercontinental missiles has considerable significance for the future.

SLBM Systems

Although we continue to have difficulty in forecasting the rate of progress of the PRC SLBM program, we remain convinced that the PRC is determined to develop a submarine-launched ballistic missile and a modern nuclear-powered ballistic missile submarine. It is estimated that the first-generation Chinese SLBM will be a solid-propellant system comparable in size to the early US Polaris missiles.

Bomber Force

PRC production of the Badger Tu-16 jet intermediate-range bomber began in 1968, but apparently ceased after some 60 of this Soviet-designed bomber were built. It is too early to determine whether production will resume. The Tu-16 was first observed in the Soviet Union in 1953 and has a combat radius of 1,650 nautical miles.

The Beagle Il-28 twin-jet short-range bomber is an old (1950) and vulnerable bomber, but the PRC military planners still appear to consider it an important weapon system. More than 400 Il-28s are now operational. The PRC may plan to equip some of these aircraft for a nuclear attack role. There are about 100 airfields in the PRC from which Il-28s could operate. Staging from those airfields closest to the border would permit strategic operations against substantial portions of the contiguous Soviet Union, all of South Korea, parts of South Vietnam, and some of India. The limited range of the aircraft suggests that it also might be used in a theater support role within the PRC.

Strategic Defense

There continues to be no indication of any PRC effort to deploy an ABM system. The PRC's air defense system remains subject to major weaknesses, including the severe shortage of all-weather interceptors, a limited number of SAM sites, and an outmoded air defense operating system.

The over 3,500 operational home defense interceptor force consists of MiG-17s, MiG-19s, and MiG-21s. The PRC has produced a number of MiG-21s, but for reasons which are not yet fully clear to us, production was suspended, and only a small number of PRC-produced MiG-21s are operational with the PRC Air Force. The balance of the operational Fishbeds were Soviet-provided some years ago. The Chinese are now developing a new all-weather interceptor of Chinese design. The PRC has a number of years of R&D effort invested in this aircraft. We had expected production of the MiG-19 to terminate, but we now believe it will continue until the new interceptor is introduced. A Chinese variant of the Soviet SA-2 missile remains the basic PRC operational SAM system. The PRC operates a relatively thin, well-organized defense, short of the massive system deployed by the USSR. The PRC has deployed a massive array of anti-aircraft artillery pieces to defend key military and industrial facilities in addition to major population centers. Our experience in Vietnam and our observation of the Middle East lead us to give this capability more consideration than we may have ten years ago. It may be concluded that, for the near term at least, the PRC will rely on size, dispersal of industrial facilities, and a modest air defense program to be its basic active defense against air attack.

Appendix B
Strategic Bomber Aircraft

Number	Name	Operational	Gross Weight	Engines[a]	Maximum Speed	Crew	Notes
US							
B-29	Superfortress	1943-54[b]	110,000 lbs	4-R	367 mph	11	3,970 built; also flown by UK
B-50	Superfortress	1948-53[c]	173,000 lbs	4-R	380 mph	11	B-50D data; 370 built
B-36	—	1948-59	357,500 lbs	6-R[d]	439 mph	16[e]	B-36D data; 325 built
B-47	Stratojet	1951-65[f]	175,000 lbs	6-TJ/7,200	606 mph	3	B-47E data; ~2,060 built
B-52	Superfortress	1955-★	448,000 lbs	8-TJ/17,000	645 mph	6	B-52H data; 448 built
B-58	Hustler	1960-69	160,000 lbs	4-TJ/15,600	1,385 mph	3	B-58A data; 104 built
B-70	Valkyrie	——	500,000 lbs	6-TJ/25,000+	2,000+ mph	4	2 built; never operational; first flight 1964
FB-111	——	1969-★	110,000 lbs	2-TJ/20,000	supersonic	2	76 built; variable-geometry wings
B-1	——	1980 est.	395,000 lbs	4-TJ/30,000	supersonic	4	under development
AJ	Savage	1949-60	55,000 lbs	2-R[g]	400 mph	3	carrier-based; 143 built

Appendix B — continued

Number	Name	Operational	Gross Weight	Engines[a]	Maximum Speed	Crew	Notes
A3D/A-3[h]	Skywarrior	1956-★	70,000 lbs	2-TJ/12,400	610 mph	3	carrier-based; data for A-3B; 285 built; survives in tanker-electronic role only
A3J/A-5[h]	Vigilante	1961-★	60,000 lbs	2-TJ/17,000	1,385 mph	2	carrier-based; approximately 150 built; recce role only
USSR							
Tu-4	BULL	1946-60	105,000 lbs	4-R	~350 mph	~10	approximately 1,200 built; also flown by China
Tu-16	BADGER	1954-★	165,000 lbs	2-TJ/19,180	620 mph	7	data for Badger-A; approximately 1,500-2,000 built; also flown by China
Tu-20	BEAR	1956-★	365,000 lbs	4-TP	550 mph	6-8	data for Bear-B; approximately 300 built
Tu-22	BLINDER	1962-★	185,000 lbs	2-TJ/26,500	925 mph	3	approximately 175-200 built
Mya-4	BISON	1956-★	365,000 lbs	4-TJ/19,180	620 mph	6-8	approximately 150 built
	BACKFIRE	1974-★	275,000 lbs	2-TJ	supersonic	2-4	variable-geometry wings

Appendix B — continued

Number	Name	Opera-tional	Gross Weight	Engines[a]	Maximum Speed	Crew	Notes
UK							
	Valiant	1955-64	175,000 lbs	4-TJ/10,050	554 mph		B Mk 1 data; 111 built
	Vulcan	1957-★	200,000 lbs	4-TJ/20,000	640 mph	5	B Mk 2 data; now used in tactical role
	Victor	1958-★	200,000 lbs	4-TJ/20,000	640 mph	5	B Mk 2 data; 76 built; now used in tanker and recce roles
	TSR-2	—	90,000+ lbs	2-TJ/30,000	supersonic	2	never operational; first flight 1964
	Buccaneer	1962-★	38,500 lbs	2-TJ/7,100	720 mph	2	S Mk 1 data; carrier based
France							
	Mirage IV-A	1964-★	73,800 lbs	2-TJ/15,435	1454 mph	2	65 built

★ currently in service
US-NATO designations for Soviet aircraft are in CAPITAL LETTERS
a R = Reciprocating
TJ = Turbojet (with maximum thrust each in pounds; includes afterburning and injection systems)
TP = Turboprop
b last B-29; some KB-29 tanker aircraft remained in service longer.
c last B-50; some RB-50 reconnaissance aircraft remained in service longer.
d four jet engines in wing pods added in B-36D.
e including 5 relief crewmen.
f last B-47; some RB-47 reconnaissance aircraft remained in service longer.
g also fitted with auxiliary jet engine.
h US aircraft designations changed in 1962.

Appendix C
Stragetic Cruise Missiles

Number	Name	Operational	Launch Weight	Engines[a]	Maximum Speed	Range	Note
US							
TM-61/MGM-1	Matador	1954-64	13,800 lbs	TJ	650 mph	600 nmi	land-launched
MGM-13	Mace	1959-70	18,000 lbs	TJ	650+ mph	1,200 nmi	land-launched; MGM-13B data
SM-62	Snark	1961	60,000 lbs	TJ	transonic	5,500 nmi	land-launched
GAM-63	Rascal[c]	—	13,000 lbs	R	supersonic	100 nmi	bomber-launched; cancelled
SM-64	Navaho	—		RJ	supersonic	5,000+ nmi	land-launched; cancelled
GAM-77/AGM-28	Hound Dog	1961-★	10,000 lbs	TJ	1,400+ mph	500+ nmi	B-52-launched
AGM-69	SRAM[b]	1972-★	2,200 lbs	R	supersonic	100 nmi	B-52/FB-111-launched
SSM-8/RGM-6	Regulus I	1953-64	12,000 lbs	TJ	500 mph	500 nmi	submarine-launched
SSM-9/RGM-15	Regulus II	—	22,000 lbs	TJ	supersonic	1,000 nmi	submarine-launched; cancelled
GAM-87	Skybolt[c]	—	11,300 lbs	R-S	supersonic		cancelled 1962

Appendix C — continued

Number	Name	Operational	Launch Weight	Engines[a]	Maximum Speed	Range	Note
USSR							
AS-2[d]	KIPPER	1961-★		TJ		100+ nmi	Badger-launched
AS-3[e]	KANGAROO	1960-★		TJ	supersonic	350 nmi	Badger/Bear-launched
AS-4[e]	KITCHEN	1967-★		TJ	supersonic	250 nmi	Blinder/Badger-launched
AS-5[e]	KELT	1965-★		R-SL	supersonic	125 nmi	Badger-launched
AS-6[e]	—	1970-★		TJ	supersonic	300 nmi	Badger-launched
SS-N-3[d]	SHADDOCK	1961-★		TJ	transonic	430 nmi	submarine-launched
UK							
	Blue Steel[c]	1962-69		R-SL	supersonic	200 nmi	Vulcan/Victor-launched; Mk 1 data

★ currently in service
US-NATO designations for Soviet missiles are in CAPITAL LETTERS
[a] TJ = Turbojet
RJ = Ramjet
R-SL = Rocket-Storable Liquid fuel
R = Rocket-solid fuel
[b] Short-Range Attack Missile
[c] ballistic *not* cruise missile; included here because of role and launch platform; the SRAM is "semi-ballistic"
[d] primarily anti-ship missile
[e] also have anti-ship capability.

Appendix D
Intercontinental Ballistic Missiles

Number	Name	Operational	Launch Weight	Length	Engines[a]	Range	Notes
US							
SM-65	Atlas	1959-65	260,000 lbs	82½ ft	R-SL	5,500 nmi	Atlas-D data
SM-68/LGM-25	Titan	1959-★	330,000 lbs	104 feet	R-SL	6,300 nmi	Titan-II data; 54 remain
SM-80/LGM-30B	Minuteman-I	1962-★	65,000 lbs	56 feet	R-S	5,500 nmi	being phased out
LGM-30F	Minuteman-II	1966-★	70,000 lbs	60 feet	R-S	6,000+ nmi	450 planned
LGM-30G	Minuteman-III	1970-★	76,000 lbs	60 feet	R-S	7,000 nmi	550 planned; 3 MIRVs
USSR							
SS-6	SAPWOOD				R-SL		
SS-7	SADDLER	1962-★		100 feet	R-SL	5,500+ nmi	
SS-8	SASIN	1963-★		80 feet	R-L	6,000 nmi	
SS-9	SCARP	1967-★		110 feet	R-SL	6,000 nmi	Mod 4 = 3 MRVs; Mod 3 = FOBS
SS-10	SCRAG	—		120 feet	R-SL	4,000+ nmi	not deployed
SS-11		1966-★		65 feet	R-SL	5,500+ nmi	Mod 3 = 3 MRVs

Appendix D — continued

Number	Name	Operational	Launch Weight	Length	Engines[a]	Range	Notes
SS-13	SAVAGE	1969-★		65 feet	R-S	5,500 nmi	
SS-X-16[b]		1975 est.			R-S	5,000+ nmi	possible MIRV
SS-17		1975 est.			R-SL	5,500+ nmi	4 MIRVs
SS-18		1975 est.			R-SL	5,500+ nmi	5-8 MIRVs
SS-19		1975 est.			R-SL	5,500+ nmi	4-6 MIRVs

★ currently in service
US-NATO designations for Soviet aircraft are in CAPITAL LETTERS
[a] R-L = Rocket-Liquid fuel
  R-SL = Rocket-Storable Liquid fuel
  R-S = Rocket-Solid fuel
[b] X in designation indicates missile in development stage.

Appendix E
Submarine-Launched Ballistic Missiles

Number	Name	Opera-tional	Launch Weight	Length	Engines[a]	Range	Notes
US							
UGM-27A	Polaris A-1	1960-65	28,000 lbs	28 ft	R-S	1,200 nmi	replaced by A-3
UGM-27B	Polaris A-2	1962-★	30,000 lbs	31 ft	R-S	1,500 nmi	being replaced by A-3
UGM-27C	Polaris A-3	1964-★	35,000 lbs	32 ft	R-S	2,500 nmi	also used by UK; 3 MRV
UGM-73A	Poseidon C-3	1971-★	65,000 lbs	34 ft	R-S	approx. 2,500 nmi	up to 14 MIRV
UGM-93A	Trident C-4	1978-est.		34 ft	R-S	approx. 4,000 nmi	estimated up to 24 MIRV at lesser ranges
	Trident D-5	indefinite			R-S	approx. 6,000 nmi	proposed
USSR							
SS-N-4	SARK	1958-★		38 ft	R-SL	350 nmi	surface launch
SS-N-5	SERB	1963-★		43 ft	R-SL	650 nmi	
SS-N-6		1968-★		30 ft	R-SL	1,300 nmi	Mod 2 = MRV and longer range
SS-N-8		1973-★		40+ ft	R-SL	4,200 nmi	
SS-N-13		1975(?)			R	350 nmi	tactical anti-ship with in-flight guidance

Appendix E — continued

Number	Name	Operational	Launch Weight	Length	Engines[a]	Range	Notes
France							
MSBS	M-1	1971-★	39,680 lbs	34 ft	R-S	1,350 nmi	
MSBS	M-2	late 1970s		34 ft	R-S	1,600 nmi	

★ currently in service
US-NATO designations for Soviet missiles are in CAPITAL LETTERS
[a] R-L = Rocket-Liquid fuel
R-SL = Rocket-Storable Liquid fuel
R-S = Rocket-Solid fuel

Appendix F
Strategic Missile Submarines

Name-Class	Number of Sub-marines	Completed	Displacement (Surface)	Length	Propulsion[a]	Missiles	Note
US							
Tunny, Barbero	2	1942, 1944	1,525 tons	312 ft	DE	2 Regulus-I	conversions
Growler, Grayback	2	1958	2,540 tons	317½ ft	DE	4 Regulus-I[b]	*Growler* data
Halibut	1	1960	3,850 tons	350 ft	Nuclear	5 Regulus-I[c]	now used for research
George Washington	5★	1960-61	5,900 tons	381½ ft	Nuclear	16 Polaris[d]	
Ethan Allan	5★	1961-63	6,900 tons	410½ ft	Nuclear	16 Polaris[e]	
Lafayette	31★	1963-67	7,320 tons	425 ft	Nuclear	16 Poseidon[f]	
Trident		1978 est.	15,000 tons	560 ft	Nuclear	24 Trident-I	10 planned
USSR							
ZULU-V	6	mid-1950s	2,000 tons	300 ft	DE	2 *SS-N-4*	conversions
GOLF	23★	1958-62	2,300 tons	320 ft	DE	3 *SS-N-4/5*[g]	1 sunk
HOTEL	9★	1958-62	3,700 tons	380 ft	Nuclear	3 *SS-N-5*[h]	
YANKEE	34★	1968-73	8,000 tons	425 ft	Nuclear	16 *SS-N-6* or *SS-N-13*	
DELTA-I	18+★	1973-	8,000+ tons	~450 ft	Nuclear	12 *SS-N-8*	
DELTA-II			8,000+ tons	~450 ft	Nuclear	16 *SS-N-8*	

Appendix F — continued

Name-Class	Number of Submarines	Completed	Displacement (Surface)	Length	Propulsion[a]	Missiles	Note
WHISKEY[1]	13	early 1950s	1,200 tons	247-275 ft	DE	1 to 4 *SS-N-3*[j]	
JULIETT[1]	16★	1961-69	2,200 tons	280 ft	DE	4 *SS-N-3*	
ECHO-I[1]	5	1960-62	4,600 tons	~380 ft	Nuclear	6 *SS-N-3*	ECHO-I converted to attack role
ECHO-II[1]	27★		5,000 tons	~385 ft	Nuclear	8 *SS-N-3*	
UK							
Resolution	4★	1967-69	7,500 tons	425 ft	Nuclear	16 Polaris A-3	
France							
LeRedoutable	5★	1971-78	7,500 tons	420 ft	Nuclear	16 MSBS	

★ currently in service
US-NATO designations for Soviet missiles are in CAPITAL LETTERS
a DE indicates diesel-electric.
b designed to carry 2 Regulus-II missiles.
c designed to carry 4 Regulus-II missiles.
d complete with Polaris A-1 missiles; rearmed with A-3.
e completed with Polaris A-2 missiles; being rearmed with A-3.
f completed with Polaris A-2 (8 submarines) or A-3 (23 submarines); all being rearmed with Poseidon C-3.
g completed with SS-N-4 missiles; 10 believed rearmed with SS-N-5.
h completed with SS-N-4 missiles; rearmed with SS-N-5.
i generally considered to have primary anti-ship role.
j 1 submarine converted to carry 1 SS-N-3 missile, 5 converted to carry 2 missiles, and 7 converted to carry 4 missiles.

Index

(Note: Appendixes B through F are not indexed below.)

159

National Strategy Information Center, Inc.

STRATEGY PAPERS

Edited by Frank N. Trager and William Henderson
With the assistance of Dorothy E. Nicolosi

Strategic Weapons: An Introduction by Norman Polmar, October 1975

Soviet Sources of Military Doctrine and Strategy by William F. Scott. July 1975

Detente: Promises and Pitfalls by Gerald L. Steibel, March 1975

Oil, Politics, and Sea Power: The Indian Ocean Vortex by Ian W. A. C. Adie, December 1974

The Soviet Presence in Latin America by James D. Theberge, June 1974

The Horn of Africa by J. Bowyer Bell, Jr., December 1973

Research and Development and the Prospects for International Security by Frederick Seitz and Rodney W. Nichols, December 1973

Raw Material Supply in a Multipolar World by Yuan-li Wu. October 1973

The People's Liberation Army: Communist China's Armed Forces by Angus M. Fraser, August 1973 (Out of print)

Nuclear Weapons and the Atlantic Alliance by Wynfred Joshua, May 1973

How to Think About Arms Control and Disarmament by James E. Dougherty, May 1973

The Military Indoctrination of Soviet Youth by Leon Goure, January 1973 (Out of print)

The Asian Alliance: Japan and United States Policy by Franz Michael and Gaston J. Sigur, October 1972

162

Iran, The Arabian Peninsula, and the Indian Ocean by R. M. Burrel and Alvin J. Cottrell, September 1972 (Out of print)

Soviet Naval Power: Challenge for the 1970s by Norman Polmar, April 1972. Revised edition, September 1974

How Can We Negotiate with the Communists? by Gerald L. Steibel, March 1972 (Out of print)

Soviet Political Warfare Techniques, Espionage and Propaganda in the 1970s by Lyman B. Kirkpatrick, Jr., and Howland H. Sargeant, January 1972

The Soviet Presence in the Eastern Mediterranean by Lawrence L. Whetten, September 1971

*The Military Unbalance
Is the U.S. Becoming a Second Class Power?* June 1971 (Out of print)

The Future of South Vietnam by Brigadier F. P. Serong, February 1971 (Out of print)

Strategy and National Interests: Reflections for the Future by Bernard Brodie, January 1971 (Out of print)

The Mekong River: A Challenge in Peaceful Development for Southeast Asia by Eugene R. Black, December 1970 (Out of print)

Problems of Strategy in the Pacific and Indian Oceans by George G. Thomson, October 1970

Soviet Penetration into the Middle East by Wynfred Joshua, July 1970. Revised edition, October 1971 (Out of print)

Australian Security Policies and Problems by Justus M. van der Kroef, May 1970 (Out of print)

Detente: Dilemma or Disaster? by Gerald L. Steibel, July 1969 (Out of print)

The Prudent Case for Safeguard by William R. Kintner, June 1969 (Out of print)

AGENDA PAPERS

Edited by Frank N. Trager and William Henderson
With the assistance of Dorothy E. Nicolosi

Seven Tracks to Peace in the Middle East by Frank R. Barnett, April 1975

Arms Treaties with Moscow: Unequal Terms Unevenly Applied? by Donald G. Brennan, April 1975

Toward a US Energy Policy by Klaus Knorr, March 1975

Can We Avert Economic Warfare in Raw Materials? US Agriculture as a Blue Chip by William Schneider, July 1974